Planning for Change:

strategic planning in local government

by

Ian Caulfield and John Schultz

General Editors: Michael Clarke and John Stewart

Longman

in association with the Local Government Training Board

Longman Group UK Limited
Longman House, Burnt Mill, Harlow, Essex CM20 2JE

First published 1989

British Library Cataloguing in Publication Data
Caufield, Ian. Schultz, John
    Planning for change: strategic planning in local government
    — (Managing local government).
    1. Great Britain. Local government.
    Corporate planning
    I. Title II. Schultz, John. III. Local Government Training
    Board IV. Series 352'.000472

ISBN 0-582-04089-2

Printed and bound in Great Britain by
Biddles Ltd, Guildford and King's Lynn

Dedication

This book is dedicated to the families we neglected while writing it!

Contents

Other titles in the series

Editors' Foreword

This book is part of a new management series launched by the *Local Government Training Board* to be published by the *Longman Group UK Ltd*. The series is designed to help those concerned with management in local government to meet the challenges of the next few years. It is based on the belief that in no period has it been so important for local authorities to have effective management.

The impact of government legislation is clear. Each local authority has to review its management, if it is to achieve an effective response. But the challenge is much deeper. In a changing society, new problems and issues demand from local authorities a capacity to respond in new ways. Local authorities have to become closer to their public as customer and citizen; resources have to be managed to achieve value in service; the requirement on all authorities is to achieve effective management of the changes which are taking place.

Effective management requires effective management development. The series is designed to aid the management development of present and future officers—and councillors. It is designed to be *used* by the reader in a variety of situations. While we hope that the books will be used on local government management courses we hope that they will have a much wider use.

They can be used by individuals or groups of managers or as the basis of seminars within authorities. However, the series will truly be a success if it becomes regarded as resource material for use in the business of management itself. We hope that the ideas discussed and the experience pooled will be a stimulus to more effective management.

The series is based on two principles. The first is the need for even greater emphasis on developing effective management in local government and the constant search for improvement. The second is that effective management must take account of the nature of local government. Need for effective management has already been stressed: the case for a separate series particular to local government is based on our second principle.

There are plenty of management books. What we have set out to produce is a series geared to the particular needs of local government. We would want to argue that those concerned with management in local government should draw on as wide a range of general experience as possible. Furthermore we would also want to argue that proper account is taken of the special purposes, conditions and tasks of local government. These books will help the manager to do just that. In publishing them we are not pretending that there is *one right way* to manage a local authority. Rather, we are exposing ideas and questions to help fashion the most helpful and effective approach to the local situation.

This book contributes to a growing series which highlights some of the key issues facing management in local authorities. The series will be extended by covering other issues of contemporary concern which require to be tackled if management — and the health of the local authority — is to be improved.

Michael Clarke, Director, Local Government Training Board
Professor John Stewart, Institute of Local Government Studies

Introduction

Our purpose

This book's sole purpose is to encourage a revival of strategic planning in local government, since we believe that strategic planning lies at the heart of bringing about the changes needed if local government is to address with success the unprecedented challenges it faces.

Of course, the theme of strategic planning is not new. It was firmly on the agenda 15 – 20 years ago. But local government and its context were very different then; and we are not advocating a return to old ways.

You will not find in this book one particular recommended model. Indeed, it is part of our contention that no 'right' way exists for all authorities, and that a reluctance to accept that was partly to blame for past difficulties. Nor will you find a learned treatise drawing on the wealth of literature, academic and otherwise, that exists on strategic planning as a generic practice.

What we have tried to do is set out some thoughts on the 'what', 'why', and 'how' of strategic planning as a vehicle for change in local government, drawing on what we consider to be encouraging examples of present practice. Many readers will undoubtedly know of other good examples.

Reader's guide

As is made clear in the Editors' Foreword, the book is meant for practitioners — managers and councillors. As far as we have been able, we have written each chapter so that it can be read individually. The key points have been summarised at the start of each chapter to help you find your way through the book and its line of argument. Each chapter ends with review questions. These are designed to encourage you to ask pertinent questions about your own authority. We hope the resulting answers will prompt debate within authorities, and help lead to action.

In Chapter 1 we sketch the changes facing local government, consider what we mean by strategic planning, and outline why we consider the latter to be crucially relevant to the former.

Chapter 2 focuses on past experience of strategic planning in local government, and attempts to draw some lessons from it.

In Chapter 3, we confront some misgivings about strategic planning and suggest some ways of overcoming resistance.

Chapter 4 lies at the heart of the book, and looks at what a strategic plan might contain.

Chapter 5 goes on to consider how to get started on the strategic planning process, and how to sustain the momentum.

Chapter 6's theme is implementation. It addresses the supporting structures, systems, and processes that can help turn a strategy into action.

In Chapter 7 we consider the topic of review: reviewing the strategy's context, and reviewing performance in achieving the strategy, so that the strategy itself can be updated.

Chapters 8–10 look at strategic planning from the point of view of councillors, officers, and the community respectively, considering the advantages that can arise for each group.

Finally, we conclude the book in Chapter 11 by arguing that success is more crucially dependent on a strategic culture than on a mechanistic process.

Acknowledgements

We should like to record our thanks to those numerous colleagues in Warwickshire County Council and other authorities who have willingly provided examples of interesting practice and helped influence our views through discussion. Without their help, this book would not have been possible. Space precludes using all the relevant examples we came across. Those we have used and which we consider to represent good practice have been attributed to the local authority concerned; other examples have not!

1 Planning for change

Key points

▲ Local government is experiencing changes that are even more significant than the establishment of new county and district councils in 1974.
▲ Further fundamental changes are in prospect.
▲ To be successful, local government needs to anticipate rather than just react to those changes.
▲ Strategic planning is essential to that process.

The challenge of change

Local government is facing a period of change that is more deep-seated and far-reaching than anything else that has happened to it since the Second World War. The pressures causing that change are various.

Legislation

The most visible cause is the spate of legislation introduced by Conservative governments since 1979; the predominant theme of this legislation has been to curtail the growth of local government as a part of the public sector. In particular, it has called into question the assumption, little challenged previously, that there are certain areas of operation within which local government should be active with little or no outside competition.

There were two early and fundamental moves in this direction after 1979. One was in the field of housing. Local authorities have, of course, never come anywhere near being monopoly providers of housing. However, within the rented sector, their role has been a dominant one, at least in much of the country. This dominance was threatened first by the Housing Act 1980, which introduced the notion of local authority tenants having the statutory right to buy their dwelling at an attractive discount. For those tenants not able or inclined to take advantage of this right, the Housing Act 1988 later provided the opportunity to transfer to a new landlord, or to have improvements carried out by a Housing Action Trust separate from the local authority.

The other early move after a Conservative government came to power in 1979 had a different thrust. For it was concerned not with local government's 'market share' in the provision of services direct to the community, but with how that market share was to be delivered. So it was that the Local Government, Planning & Land Act 1980 introduced the concept of making it compulsory for authorities to tender against the private sector to carry out much of their own highways and building work. However, the real momentum in the direction of compulsory competition came with the Local Government Act 1988, which extended it to vehicle maintenance, catering, cleaning of buildings, grounds maintenance, and refuse collection — and left the door open for the Secretary of State for the Environment to add other functions to the list. Sports and leisure facilities are to be the first such additional function, affected from 1992.

Far-reaching legislation has kept on coming. The Education Reform Act 1988 is accelerating the trend towards local management of schools and colleges of further education — a trend that had already begun in a range of pilot schemes throughout the country. However, the Act is to give governing bodies, headteachers, and college principals more autonomy than local government itself was contemplating. Moreover, the power given to parents to insist that children attend the school of their choice — providing space is available — and the facility for schools to opt out of local authority control are introducing a degree of customer choice that is quite new to the education service.

As with housing, local government's role in the social services field has never been a monopolistic one. The private and voluntary sectors are major participants in the provision of residential and day care. But many people have nevertheless looked to local authorities as the main providers. This view is increasingly being challenged. Perhaps most significantly, the 1988 report by Sir Roy Griffiths on community care recommended that local authorities should 'act...as the designers, organisers and purchasers of non-health care services, and not primarily as direct providers'. If this view is accepted by the government (which commissioned the report) and carried forward into legislation, the local authority role will be different, although not diminished.

The government's policy of limiting the size of the public sector has not surprisingly had an impact on local government finance. From April 1990 (one year earlier in Scotland), domestic rates are to be replaced by the community charge. From the same date, non-domestic rates will be set at a uniform level nationally. Once the complicating factor of a four-year transitional period is over (during which the effect of the changes will not be fully felt), the amount of income for which local authorities themselves set the level will fall to about one quarter from its present level of around 60%. Central government will be responsible for determining the level of the bulk of local government income via the non-domestic rate and revenue support grant. At most, these government-determined sources of income are expected to rise by the rate of retail price inflation.

It therefore follows that every extra pound in spending will need to be found by local government from local community charge payers. This will mean that (after the transitional period) every extra pound in spending over and above retail price inflation will require an extra £3–£4 to be raised from community charge payers. Allied to changes in capital controls, which are expected to limit the use of capital receipts for new capital investment, the pressures on spending to maintain or improve services will become even sharper, and the search for other more efficient ways of doing things will have to become even more concentrated.

Although some of these changes were introduced soon after 1979, the pace of legislation has accelerated since the mid-1980s. The cumulative effect has been:

▽ to put the individual in a new and stronger relationship with his or her county or district council
▽ to make local government increasingly one of a number of competing providers of services
▽ more generally, to expand contractual arrangements with voluntary and private agencies to do some of what local government did previously
▽ to emphasise local government's responsibility for quality control of other agencies' work.

Social change

The changes being brought about by the flow of legislation mask factors that were already pushing hard at what local government does and how it operates.

Up to about 20 years ago, few people challenged the consensus view that local authorities were an important focus of local aspirations. Despite more recent pressures to see councils as no more than the deliverers of a collection of specific services, many in local government have commendably stuck to the view that local authorities are more than the sum of their parts. And associated with that view has been an approach that attempts to look to the greater good of the local community as a whole. That is a strength that must not be lost; but the danger is that it can degenerate into a paternalistic outlook that pays scant regard to the place of the individual as citizen, client, or consumer. And this is what has tended to happen.

Recently, however, generally increasing wealth and education have made people in the community more sophisticated and discriminating. There has also been what has been described as 'the decline of deference'. High Street retailers — and service industry overall — have responded to this trend by moving from the 'pile it high — sell it cheap' philosophy to one that values and cares for customers as individuals. The same people are local government's customers too. They were beginning to draw uncomfortable comparisons between the services being offered by the public and private sectors. Local government professionals have traditionally prided themselves on delivering high-quality services; but members of the public were beginning to redefine 'quality' to include matters such as being treated considerately at reception desks, and having a say in their own destiny. Local government's consumer revolution had therefore already begun.

Demographic shifts were also playing their part. Rapidly increasing numbers of elderly people — an increase of nearly 30% in numbers of people aged 75 or over between 1976 and 1986 — have put services (social services in particular) under strain, and a further increase of nearly 15% is forecast by 1996. At the same time, the 'baby boom' of the 1960s has already worked its way through secondary schools, leaving in its wake:

▽ problems of large-scale surplus capacity
▽ competition for pupils — or even survival — between secondary schools
▽ competition between secondary schools and further education colleges
▽ competition between the world of education and the world of work.

Furthermore, the drop in school-leavers (expected to be around 30% over the period 1987–1995) promises even more acute recruitment difficulties for local government, which is already suffering from a lack of competitiveness in a whole range of professions.

Finally, economic recovery has brought development pressures, particularly in the southern half of Britain, but is passing many other areas by — notably certain inner cities.

Changing roles

Local government is therefore in the throes of changes that are probably more fundamental than previous changes in structure or functions. They are more fundamental because they are not just about:

▽ which particular functions local government is responsible for
▽ which combination of functions should be exercised by a particular category of authority
▽ where a particular authority's boundary should fall;

but rather about:

▽ general approach
▽ mode of operation
▽ nature of relationships with the outside world.

Moreover, change will not end here. Already the future niche of local government is emerging as:

▽ the securer but not necessarily the provider of services
▽ the enabler or facilitator — helping to make things happen. Many local authorities have been quick to seize the initiative through enterprising and entrepreneurial partnerships with the private and voluntary sectors and also other public sector agencies. Such partnerships are the foretaste of more to come.
▽ the quality-controller of services provided by the private or voluntary sectors (building on present roles in relation to, for instance, private elderly persons' homes and waste disposal facilities).

Perhaps more tentatively, one can even see the foundations being laid for the re-emergence of the role referred to earlier in this chapter:

▽ the voice of the local community — arguing, shaping, and influencing for the benefit of local people.

Local government is only at the beginning of a period of fundamental change.

Planning for change

How ready is local government to rise above the challenges, and to reshape its role so that local communities continue to see it as vital to their quality of life? To be prepared, it must think ahead and plan for change.

There are many excuses that may be used as reasons for not planning for change.

▽ Local government seems to be in a perennial financial crisis that demands short-term action, encourages defensiveness, and discourages an objective review of priorities.

▽ Busy and hard-pressed managers always have enough problems — financial or otherwise — to contend with, so that preoccupation with day-to-day management becomes an end it itself.

▽ The gamut of controls over local government spending are in a state of constant flux. Making forecasts of spending and income is, at best, hazardous. As the County Treasurer of Hampshire stated in 1988 in relation to a forecast of government grant for 1989–90, 'Health warning: indiscriminate use of these figures could damage your reputation'!

▽ Throughout local government there is the deeply-held misconception that change and uncertainty render planning impossible.

▽ Councillors are concerned that planning is dominated by officers, and frustrates political ambition.

▽ The recent increase in the number of local authorities with no overall political control adds a new dimension of uncertainty which is used to argue against the desirability and practicality of a longer-term view.

▽ The culture of the 'professional' in local government has made it harder to inject strategic thinking into management.

However, society is changing. Society's changes are driving changes in local government. The broad direction of change is inevitable, and the momentum relentless. Conservative governments have played — and continue to play — a part; but the trends are too deep-seated for a future change in government wholly to relieve the pressure. For the need for change is acknowledged right the way across the political spectrum. For example, a Fabian Society pamphlet ('Socialism, Merit and Efficiency') has argued that the structure of public services needs to be changed so that they no longer 'treat people as a potentially recalcitrant mass'. Local government must gear itself up for change. Strategic planning is a major means of facing change successfully. Major change cannot be brought about overnight, but requires concerted, purposeful action over a period.

An industrial commentator observed in 1988 that the companies that will go into the third millennium as success stories are those that have views about where they want their businesses to be in the year 2000, and not those that are obsessed with next quarter's profit target. The short-sighted equivalent for local government is the tendency to chug along as before. As John Barratt, formerly Chief Executive of Cambridgeshire County Council, put it in an unpublished paper, 'councils tend to "run" services rather than "achieve results"; officers tend to "administer" rather than "manage"'.

Such an approach was perhaps more tenable at a time when people were content to see local authorities as little more than a collection of largely self-contained services, and when the external world seemed stable. But such conditions no longer prevail. The need for strategic planning is therefore as pressing in local government as in the private sector. Unless it anticipates change, prepares for change, and is ready to change and develop its own outlook, relationships, management structures, and organisation, local government's future is bleak. As the story of the Cheshire Cat in 'Alice in Wonderland' reveals — if you do not know where you are going, it does not matter which way you go! For local government it is a short step from there to not mattering at all.

What is strategic planning?

Strategic planning means a local authority establishing its purpose and direction. That clearly embraces political purpose and direction.

The definition of strategic planning is difficult to capture in a few words. As the Audit Commission has made clear, it is emphatically not just a set of financial and manpower projections.

'Strategic' means:

▽ taking a broader view, tackling broader issues rather than getting bogged down in fine detail

▽ examining issues that are seen as important for the authority as a whole and the community it serves. Of course, that does not rule out major issues affecting only one service or department if the scale is such as to have a substantial impact on the organisation as a whole.

▽ being concerned with inter-connected issues, and those that have an impact beyond their own immediate effect.

'Planning' means:

▽ lifting sights beyond day-to-day problems and tasks
▽ translating political purpose into a sense of direction
▽ gearing up to bring about changes
▽ attempting to foresee changes
  —in the national and international context
  —in the economic environment
  —in the social environment
▽ attempting to prepare for predictable changes — like the decline in the numbers of secondary school pupils and school-leavers
▽ preparing mentally for the certainty that there will be other, unforeseen changes of some sort
▽ exploring options, choices, and contingencies
▽ confronting priority choices
▽ recognising the need for changes in management and organisation
▽ being flexible and able to accommodate change — rather than being an obstacle to responding to change.

Breaking new ground?

The product of strategic planning is a strategy or strategic plan. There are some notable examples in contemporary local government but they are not widespread.

Much more common are policy statements for particular services which:

▽ describe current circumstances but fail to look forward
▽ are seldom reviewed before they are overtaken by events
▽ are little concerned with their wider impact.

Even where local authorities have prepared genuine forward-looking policy plans for particular services, they all too rarely:

▽ relate their activities to other services

▽   observe realistic limits on the likely availability of financial and other resources
▽   recognise that they are competing with other services in the authority's priorities
▽   add up to more than 'what we will do if and when the money becomes available'.

Many authorities have medium-term plans for capital spending. However, these frequently are:

▽   not based on explicit political decisions about priorities between services
▽   inconsistent with revenue spending priorities
▽   not grounded in policy review.

A growing number of authorities have produced medium-term plans covering revenue as well as capital expenditure. When set in a wider context that includes a strategic view of where an authority is going, these can be a most valuable way of translating strategy into action. All too often, however, that context is lacking; and many medium-term plans are little more than:

▽   projections of the levels of spending necessary to sustain the present pattern of services, based on assumptions about the receipt of government grants

or else

▽   lists of desirable developments, loosely linked to likely resource availability, but giving little clue as to where the authority is heading.

If there is a strategy in these cases, it is often concealed by the detail of the planning process.

Planning of these limited sorts can clearly be very useful to the local authorities where it is progressing. Moreover, it can help create both the climate and processes for moving towards wholehearted strategic planning. But it is not enough on its own.

The Audit Commission has put strategy somewhere between vision and management structures and processes, defining it as 'those major initiatives that a council proposes to take in response to, or in anticipation of, changes in its external environment ... to achieve its vision of what it is trying to do or become' ('Improving Economy, Efficiency, and Effectiveness in Local Government in England and Wales', Volume One). Where, then, does vision give way to strategy, and strategy to management systems? Examples of good practice reveal a variety of different patterns, and variety in the use of terminology. A strategy may be clearly in evidence without being set out in a document on its own. What is important is to have all the elements present, whatever they are called. For strategy and tactics without vision are means without an end; a succinct vision cannot be turned straight into something tactical; and vision and strategy will achieve nothing if not made operational.

What more has strategic planning to offer?

The significance of strategic planning is that it lies at the heart of change in the local authority as a whole. The challenges facing local government in the late

1980s are such that all departments are affected and must be involved. What is more, many departments are affected in similar ways. Competition, choice, changing relationships between support services and sharp-end functions, changing roles — all have implications across the whole range of council services. A corporate approach to change is therefore needed more than ever.

Strategic planning can be instrumental by:

▽ encouraging a forward-looking approach
▽ preparing people for the prospect of change
▽ clarifying choices
▽ marshalling priorities in a way that shapes the response to external change
▽ pulling the threads together corporately
▽ communicating to staff a sense of purpose
▽ helping the community to understand the pressures on the local authority and what it is striving to do.

But strategic planning is unlikely to exist on its own: it is likely to be just one expression of strategic management in an authority. And strategic management requires strategic thinking, strategic leadership (by members, the chief executive, and chief officers) and strategic organisation. Forms of organisation are discussed in Chapters six and seven; but the fundamental point is that organisation must be subordinate to strategy: traditional forms of organisation can all too easily thwart both the preparation of a strategy and its implementation.

The essence

'Effective strategies concentrate resources and management attention on a few critical thrusts which cohesively integrate the entity's major goals' (Quinn, 'Strategies for Change'). The kind of strategic planning described in this book is therefore concerned with the local authority as a whole. It goes beyond the production of strategies for individual services, valuable though those usually are. It requires a certain sort of organisational culture. But it is not a straightforward, technical process. On the contrary, there are as many ways of skinning a strategic cat as there are local authorities; and finding the appropriate way for a particular council may well call for the highest level of political and managerial skills.

Review questions

▲ How well is your authority squaring up to the changes facing it?
▲ How willing is it to acknowledge emerging changes in its role?
▲ Where strategic thinking does exist, does it go beyond — and integrate — individual services?

2 Restoring strategic planning's reputation

Key points

▲ For many people in local government, strategic planning is synonymous with corporate planning or structure planning.
▲ Corporate planning is perceived as having failed.
▲ Structure planning is also seen as having serious shortcomings.
▲ The reputation of strategic planning in general therefore tends to suffer, even though it is not the principles of strategic planning that are at fault, but the way they have been applied.
▲ Recent years, however, have seen some notable attempts at reviving strategic planning in local government.

A discouraging history

This book is primarily concerned with why and how to embark on strategic planning now. But a brief foray into the past is necessary if old mistakes are not to be repeated.

For some considerable time, strategic planning has not been viewed enthusiastically within much of local government. Why should this be so? Two reasons spring to mind:

▽ For some people, strategic planning means corporate planning as practised during the 1970s.
▽ For others, strategic planning means structure planning as carried out within planning departments.

Confirmation that corporate planning has a tarnished reputation is not hard to find. One need look no further than titles: job titles, work unit titles, and conference titles. A decade or more ago, the words 'corporate planning' were widespread. Today, few local government officers are called 'Corporate Planning Officer'; few sections operate under the name of 'Corporate Planning Section'; and the former Corporate Planning Workshop hosted by Birmingham University's Institute of Local Government Studies was recently retitled 'The Local Government Management Workshop'.

Structure planning is still with us — just. However, it has come under sustained criticism over a long period; it disappeared in metropolitan areas with the demise of the metropolitan county councils; and Government proposals to replace it elsewhere by the production of county policy statements are still firmly on the agenda.

Of course, for those who are attempting to encourage strategic planning within local government, neither old-style corporate planning nor structure planning provides an adequate model, but the problem is that strategic planning in general is tarred with the same brush. Nevertheless, the 1980s have seen some attempts to persuade local government to revive strategic planning. Some authorities have responded. But those who would claim to be seriously in the strategic planning business are still not numerous; and those who have some real progress to show are fewer still.

Corporate planning

Corporate planning began to take root in British local government from around the mid to late 1960s. The twin principles — having an internal unity of purpose, and being forward-looking — were both contrary to tradition: most local authorities had been little more than a loose collection of separate services; and all too little had been done to anticipate change. These two principles — and especially the former — were enthusiastically advocated by the Committee on Management of Local Government, whose 1967 report (the Maud Report) proposed some fundamental changes in the way local authorities organised themselves. Most notably, the Committee argued for:

▽ co-ordination of the work of individual committees
▽ co-ordination of the work of officers, through a more powerful clerk or chief executive and a management team of chief officers.

The Maud Report proved very influential. A number of authorities adopted the ideas set out in it and reorganised their structures accordingly, in many cases with the aid of management consultants.

But there was clearly more to corporate planning than just organisational structure: it required a process of some sort. In this area, American experience was heavily drawn on, and there were many examples of local authorities experimenting with planning-programme-budgeting systems (PPBS) — again encouraged by management consultants. These systems encouraged:

▽ the grouping of an authority's activities into a limited number of 'programme areas', which by no means always coincided with traditional service definitions
▽ a clear statement of the authority's objectives within each of those programme areas
▽ the structuring of the authority's budget under programme area headings
▽ the consideration of alternative solutions
▽ an attempt to measure results.

They tended to draw on large quantities of data and on analytical techniques.

Further encouragement to adopt the new-style structures emerged in the 1972 Bains Report, aimed at post-reorganisation councils ('The New Local Authorities — Management and Structure'). So, by the mid 1970s, policy and resources committees, chief officers' management teams, and chief executives were commonplace, as were new, combined departments based on programme areas. Corporate planning processes such as those based on programme budgeting were still in evidence also. Yet by the end of the decade, there was widespread disillusion with corporate planning as a concept.

What went wrong?

One of the strengths of local government is its diversity: no two authorities are identical. It is no doubt true to say that, by the same token, no two authorities shared identical reasons for the decline of corporate planning. It can therefore be rather dangerous to generalise, since there will always be authorities for whom general reasons do not hold good. Nevertheless, commentators do seem to have identified some common strands, which can be grouped under four headings.

OVER-ENTHUSIASM

Much about the way local government pursued corporate planning reflects a somewhat uncritical acceptance of other people's ideas. There were, admittedly, strong pressures pushing in this direction, with the same basic messages emerging from official reports, management consultants, and experiments in government departments. Nevertheless:

▽ there was widespread, almost slavish, adoption of the possible councillor and officer structures set out in the Bains Report — right down to titles and job descriptions. However valid the underlying principles, one might have expected their translation into practice to have reflected local government's traditional diversity to a much greater extent.
▽ the faithful copying of structures may not have done much harm in itself, but it spelled real trouble when mirrored in the copying of processes. In some authorities, the potential benefits to be found in the underlying principles of, for example, programme budgeting were eventually lost from view as the emphasis was put on the mechanics of a particular version of it.
▽ with similar over-enthusiasm, some authorities tried to run before they could walk.

In the prophetic words of Tony Eddison, 'corporate planning runs the danger of becoming the thing no self-respecting local authority should admit to being without... The great temptation is to leap into the mechanics and organisational structure' ('Local Government: Management and Corporate Planning').

LOSS OF STRATEGIC VIEW

The hierarchy of objectives required in programme budgeting was designed to give a co-ordinated overview. It is therefore somewhat ironic that the corporate planning processes adopted in many local authorities led to the eclipse of such a strategic view through attempts to be:

▽ too comprehensive: covering all of a council's activities
▽ too detailed: one consultant's report amounted to a corporate planning manual of nearly 300 pages

▽   too sophisticated: many descriptions of PPBS were complicated and full of unfamiliar jargon.

So it was that, in some authorities, corporate planning processes became characterised by:

▽   an emphasis on form filling
▽   vast quantities of paper
▽   information overload
▽   a failure to discriminate between:
      —the crucial and the less important
      —the strategic and the detailed
      —areas of change and areas of stability.

In the circumstances, it is perhaps little wonder that corporate planning began to lose credibility, and seemed decreasingly relevant.

LACK OF COMMITMENT

Although restructured in a way that was designed to facilitate corporate planning, many authorities nevertheless encountered organisational difficulties.

▽   As a general rule, corporate planning was driven by the centre of the organisation. All too little attention was devoted to securing support from front-line departments.
▽   There was little recognition that understanding and support from officers required a degree of culture change, which in turn required some sort of management development.
▽   Even more seriously, too little attention was paid to securing and retaining councillor commitment. Any such commitment could rapidly wane as exercises became excessively technical, with little scope for political vision.
▽   Nor was there likely to be wider public interest in, or support for, processes that appeared to focus predominantly on an authority itself rather than also on impact on the community — despite the underlying rationale of processes such as programme budgeting being just the opposite.

LINKS WITH GROWTH

It is no coincidence that corporate planning was introduced in a period of growth and reached its low point in a period of recession. The Bains Report combined a belief in corporate working with a belief that local authorities were responsible for the overall well-being of the local area — not just for delivering a limited range of services. This broad view was easier to sustain at a time when expenditure was rising rapidly, and sat comfortably with corporate planning processes concerned with how to target additional money most effectively. What is more, the processes themselves were hardly cheap to operate.

Perhaps ironically, more recent variants of the former corporate planning processes have been introduced as means of tackling resource scarcity, as described in Chapter 7. But this was not the emphasis in the 1970s; and the end of rapidly expanding budgets helped seal the fate of corporate planning processes towards the end of the decade.

Structure planning

Just as, for some, the term 'strategic planning' summons up recollections of corporate planning, so for others the association is with structure planning.

Structure planning found its way into English and Welsh local government in 1971, as a result of the Planning Act of 1968, at much the same time as corporate planning surfaced in many authorities. Structure plans were intended to fulfil seven functions:

▽   interpreting national and regional policies
▽   establishing aims, policies, and general proposals (for the development and use of land)
▽   providing the framework for local plans
▽   indicating action areas
▽   providing guidance for development control
▽   providing the basis for co-ordinating decisions
▽   bringing main planning issues and decisions before the Minister and public (Development Plans — a manual of form and content).

Structure planning is therefore narrower than corporate planning in the sense that it focuses on only one element of a local authority's activities: land use planning and associated matters. In another sense, though, it is wider, as it is also concerned with the actions of agencies wholly independent of the local authority itself. Both, however, belong to the strategic planning family.

After only six years, a House of Commons sub-committee was calling for a review of the development plans system of which structure plans were a major component. Partly because so few structure plans had passed through all the formal stages required, the Government considered such a review to be premature. However, with the abolition of the metropolitan county councils in 1985, structure planning in metropolitan areas was replaced by the Secretary of State's strategic guidance; and a Government consultation paper published in 1986 ('The Future of Development Plans') proposed the replacement of structure plans in shire areas with statements of county policies, coupled with district-wide local plans. This proposal was reiterated in a White Paper early in 1989. The end could well be in sight for structure planning as it exists today.

What went wrong?

Much of what went wrong with structure planning sounds a more general warning note for other types of strategic planning. Among the shortcomings identified in the Government's consultation paper were slowness of completion and unnecessary length.

SLOWNESS OF COMPLETION

It took 14 years to complete the first full cycle of structure plans for England and Wales; and by 1985 the average period for producing a structure plan and securing its approval by the Secretary of State was estimated to average nearly five years. By the time the lengthy survey researches were complete, they were often out of date. And plans themselves had often been all but overtaken by events by the time of formal approval. Nor was formal amendment a materially quicker process: the same general procedures had to be complied with.

UNNECESSARY LENGTH

The inordinate length of some structure plans, it was claimed, stemmed from the inclusion of inappropriate detail. Several plans exceeded 100,000 words, containing over 100 policies.

These characteristics lead to a further shortcoming: lack of responsiveness to change.

LACK OF RESPONSIVENESS TO CHANGE

Despite avowed intentions to the contrary, structure plans have tended to take on the nature of 'blueprints'. It is hardly surprising if, faced with a newly-approved plan already showing signs of obsolescence, and further faced with a seemingly interminable process to secure its formal amendment, county planning authorities have tended to adhere to structure plan policies with a degree of obstinacy. The problem has been compounded by the long time-horizon of 15 years.

Extraordinarily, the importance of being responsive to change seems to have been seriously under-estimated, despite structure planning's birth in a period of major change. The Government's Development Plans Manual is at best lukewarm about the need: 'if, later, new information calls this proposal into question ... there may be a case for an alteration to the approved structure plan'.

Structure plans, then, have been seriously — perhaps fatally — flawed by their inadequacy at dealing with:

▽   differences between forecasts and what actually happens
▽   changing aspirations in society
▽   the unexpected.

The Government's consultation paper identified a further two problems with structure planning: the inclusion of irrelevant matters, not relating to land-use planning, and overlap with matters in local plans.

INCLUSION OF IRRELEVANT MATTERS/OVERLAP WITH MATTERS IN LOCAL PLANS

County planning authorities would no doubt express these issues in a different way, and would state that the rules prescribed by central government were not always appropriate on the ground.

LACK OF LINKS WITH OTHER TYPES OF PLAN

In theory, structure plans should be closely aligned with other local authority plans and, indeed, other government plans. But, given the lack of responsiveness to change already identified, it became inevitable that discrepancies would develop, as other types of plan responded more quickly to changing circumstances. Potentially most serious of all is the lack of firm links to the availability of finance, both public and private.

Recent signs of life

Despite the shortcomings in practice of both corporate planning and structure planning, and despite the resulting damage to the reputation of strategic planning in general, the 1980s have seen the revival of external pressures on local authorities to reintroduce some form of authority-wide strategic planning.

▽ Early in the decade, journal articles by management consultants and accountants extolling the virtues of strategic planning in the public sector became more common. Much was no doubt owed to lessons from the private sector, where successive oil crises and the economic fall-out from them put a premium on planning to respond to uncertainty. Successful companies were those that had learned to cope with change and live with it. Living with it meant looking ahead and a strong revival for company strategic planning. Perhaps not surprisingly, the impetus given to public sector strategic planning by the commercial world placed an undue emphasis on the financial element of planning, and political considerations tended to be neglected.

▽ Perhaps the most persistent source of pressure has been the Audit Commission. The first volume of its handbook 'Improving Economy, Efficiency, and Effectiveness in Local Government in England & Wales', published in 1983, identified strategy as one of the seven basic elements necessary to secure the good overall management of a local authority.

▽ More recently, the Commission's Management Paper entitled 'The Competitive Council' stated 'any council wishing to shape its future in a positive fashion must operate a simple but effective policy planning system'.

▽ Taking their lead from the Audit Commission, external auditors now make a habit of exhorting authorities to adopt strategic planning if they have not already done so.

▽ The Local Government Training Board has concentrated on encouragement rather than pressure, with its papers designed to stimulate good practice (e.g. 'Going for Better Management', 'Managing Tomorrow', and 'The Enabling Council').

Whether in response to such external pressures, or just for internal reasons, an increasing number of authorities have started to reintroduce some form of authority-wide strategic planning, with varying degrees of success. Examples of these appear in later chapters.

Lessons to be learned

What, then, are the lessons from history as far as strategic planning in local government is concerned? The following pointers seem to emerge:

▽ start with something modest rather than over-ambitious
▽ avoid over-sophistication

∇   be highly selective about research
∇   don't adopt something slavishly from elsewhere: tailor something to your
    own authority
∇   keep paper within manageable bounds
∇   be selective about issues to include
∇   ensure that the strategic plan is relevant to the real world
∇   emphasise vision as well as process
∇   ensure that the plan is firmly rooted in politics
∇   gain commitment from beyond the centre of the organisation
∇   attach considerable importance to gaining councillor commitment
∇   focus on both the organisation and the environment
∇   reflect the fact that change now rarely means growth
∇   reflect realistic resource availability
∇   avoid a blueprint approach
∇   adopt a workable time horizon
∇   build in regular reviews as a vital part of the process.

These themes are developed in later chapters.

Review questions

∇   To what extent does strategic planning in your own authority suffer from a
    poor reputation inherited from the past?
∇   Is your authority geared up to avoid past mistakes in approaching the
    preparation of strategic plans?
∇   Is your authority embarking on strategic planning in its own way and not
    following slavishly the ideas and suggestions of others?

3 Gaining support

Key points

▲ A vital step in the process of introducing strategic planning is gaining support for it.
▲ This entails understanding why some people start out less than keen on the idea.
▲ Support should be sought from councillors, officers, and the public.

A sound idea is not enough

Local government is local democracy, and that means politics. As the Widdicombe Report ('Report of the Committee of Inquiry into the Conduct of Local Authority Business') showed, local authorities where party politics is not firmly entrenched are a declining if not endangered species. And, of course, politics is the art of the possible — not of the necessary or the appropriate. It follows that there is far more to introducing a sound idea into a local authority than merely extolling its virtues. This is certainly true of strategic planning. A key step has to be to gain support — and, indeed, to retain it; and to do this requires the identification and addressing of the underlying reasons for resistance.

Councillor attitudes

In late 1982, Arun District Council appointed a new chief executive with a clear brief to manage the Authority in a corporate manner under political direction. One of the first results was a joint — political and managerial — analysis of the Authority's problems, which were summed up as 'above all, failure to establish purpose and direction' (Arun District Council: 'Framework of Overall Arrangements for the Effective and Efficient Management of its Business Affairs').

This is a good example of the underlying drive for strategic planning coming from councillors — or, at the very least, of councillors setting in train a managerial revolution of which some form of strategic planning was an inescapable element. Arun is not unique. Parallels exist in Kent County Council, which appointed a new chief executive in 1986 in broadly similar circumstances.

Much more commonly, however, it is officers who come forward with proposals to embark on strategic planning. Sometimes the idea is warmly welcomed: on occasion, councillors are sufficiently enthusiastic to intervene actively in moulding the basic idea into a process which meets their view of what is needed. This has been true of Avon County Council, where member involvement in redesigning the policy and performance review activities since 1986 has been very far from passive.

On the other hand, many readers will all too readily identify with those councils where it is hard work to persuade councillors of the value of embarking on a strategic planning process. Why is this state of affairs so common? Central to the answer must be the general differences of perspective and perception between so many councillors on the one hand and officers on the other. Officers must therefore do their best to see things from the point of view of councillors if they are not to jeopardise the successful introduction of strategic planning.

How, then, do councillors perceive strategic planning? Commonly encountered views include the following.

'STRATEGIC PLANNING WILL RESTRICT OUR POLITICAL FREEDOM OF ACTION.'

Many councillors see planning and flexibility as incompatible. Declaring, openly and publicly, direction and targets for the local authority for several years ahead is regarded as a political straitjacket. There is real concern that the inevitable and essential manoeuvring within those overall policies will be viewed as political weakness or even cowardice.

'IF OUR GOALS ARE EXPLICIT, ANY FAILURE TO ACHIEVE THEM WILL BE ALL TOO CLEAR.'

One County Council party leader remarked that preparing a strategic plan was akin to setting an examination paper for yourself that you were bound to fail. No council would achieve everything it set out to do. To publish intentions in a strategic plan simply highlights failure.

'IF OUR GOALS ARE EXPLICIT, IT WILL BE EASIER FOR OTHERS TO THWART US.'

Those others need not be party-political opponents, of course: they can be pressure groups in the community. Representatives from at least one council have been heard to admit that they were quite successful at closing surplus schools — until they announced a policy of doing so!

'STRATEGIC PLANNING HELPS OFFICERS GAIN THE UPPER HAND.'

This suspicion is fostered when strategic planning is presented as a predominantly technical activity, at best apolitical, and at worst anti-political. Moreover, the more paper and process involved, the less likely are members to feel in control and to benefit.

'STRATEGIC PLANNING IS FINE IN THEORY, BUT NOT IN PRACTICE.'

Some councillors, particularly those with lengthy experience of being in the controlling party of an authority, look back on what they see as a perfectly satisfactory state of affairs in the past, and see no need for what they consider to be new-style management ideas. Some may even regard the proposal to introduce strategic planning as an implied criticism of their own stewardship in the past.

'ANY SORT OF PLANNING IS IMPOSSIBLE IN A COUNCIL WITH NO OVERALL MAJORITY.'

There is a widespread view that there can be little confidence in future voting patterns within a council if one political party does not command the majority of votes, and that there can therefore be little confidence that any plan will be adhered to. At the very best, compromise decisions would undermine a plan. All in all, so the argument runs, planning is not worth wasting time on in such circumstances.

'STRATEGIC PLANNING IS ACTUALLY POLITICALLY UNDESIRABLE IN A COUNCIL WITH NO OVERALL MAJORITY.'

Operating in such councils requires political adroitness. It rarely suits any party to become too closely identified with another over a sustained period. Formal coalitions are resisted — and so is too much publicly-visible agreement over strategy.

'STRATEGIC PLANNING MIGHT WORK ELSEWHERE — BUT IT WOULDN'T WORK HERE.'

The 'yes — but...' culture is perhaps the most difficult to break down. It is an expression of a negative philosophy, disguised by superficial intent, and every organisation has at least a significant minority of such people.

'WHAT WORKS IN THE PRIVATE SECTOR ISN'T ALWAYS APPROPRIATE IN LOCAL GOVERNMENT.'

This is a truism. But equally an approach that has helped and is helping the private sector to climb out of deep recession and uncertainty must offer principles that can be of assistance to local government which is experiencing radical change of similar magnitude.

Officer attitudes

It would, of course, be wholly mistaken to conclude that the only resistance to the introduction of strategic planning comes from councillors. This is far from the case. Indeed, it would not be far off the mark to say that scepticism is still endemic in much of local government's officer structure. Any strategic planning initiative therefore clearly needs to consider how to gain officer commitment in addition to councillor support. This suggests a need to take stock of common officer objections.

'I'VE SEEN IT ALL BEFORE: STRATEGIC PLANNING DIDN'T WORK THEN, AND IT WON'T WORK NOW.'

As suggested in Chapter 2, attitudes are jaundiced by past experiences. The real message, however, is that strategic planning has to learn from those mistakes.

'STRATEGIC PLANNING WOULDN'T WORK WITH OUR COUNCILLORS.'

Taken at face value, this should represent a challenge, not an excuse for doing nothing. Too often, however, the statement means a lack of enthusiasm and commitment on the part of the officer.

'I'M TOO BUSY RUNNING A SERVICE.'

This argument is difficult to gainsay. However, there is also a great deal of comfort and security in the routine. Managers must 'stick their heads above the parapet' on a regular basis to make sure that what they are doing is still right and relevant.

'SO MUCH IS CHANGING IN LOCAL GOVERNMENT TODAY — A STRATEGIC PLAN WOULDN'T HOLD GOOD FOR FIVE MINUTES.'

This is a view that will strike sympathetic chords with many. But it is also true that without vision and direction local government itself may not last very long.

'THE GOVERNMENT'S PERPETUAL MOVING OF THE FINANCIAL GOAL POSTS MAKES STRATEGIC PLANNING IMPOSSIBLE.'

It certainly makes it difficult, but paradoxically represents one of the main reasons why a longer-term view is needed.

'THE IDEA IS BEING CHAMPIONED BY CENTRAL DEPARTMENTS — AND THEY DON'T UNDERSTAND WHAT'S RELEVANT AT THE SHARP END.'

If that criticism is valid, strategic planning is failing. The purpose behind it is to assist and support the delivery of services. Moreover, some of the more successful recent forays into strategic planning have begun in service departments.

Public attitudes

The general public is inevitably at one remove from decisions on matters such as a strategic planning process. It would therefore be easy to dismiss as irrelevant any link between public attitudes and the question of whether or not to embark on strategic planning. This could, however, prove somewhat short-sighted for a number of reasons.

▽ Opinion polls repeatedly show that the public as a whole is woefully ignorant of local government. At the most basic level, a large proportion of people have at best a hazy idea even of what local government exists to do. The complex split of functions between local government and the rest of the public sector, between tiers of local government, and between councils in metropolitan and shire areas exacerbates the problem — but is not wholly responsible for it.

▽ It follows that, if a council does not impinge on its public sufficiently to get across the message about what role it performs, the public is hardly likely to identify with it, support it, or be influenced by it.

▽ By contrast, the authority that manages to reach people with a clear message about what it stands for and where it is going is more likely to have an impact with the public — although not everyone will agree with the content of the message, of course!

▽ What is more, a council is more likely to create a favourable impression with at least certain sections of the outside world if it is demonstrably well managed — and developing a strategy is increasingly seen as an inescapable element of good management.

Ideas on gaining support

The best way to gain support is, of course, to demonstrate the benefits in practice. What the benefits of strategic planning could turn out to be is a topic considered in Chapters eight to ten. The problem is to win people over before the benefits can be seen! But taking account of the commonly encountered attitudes noted earlier can provide some pointers to possible ways forward.

ENSURE THAT BOTH COUNCILLORS AND OFFICERS UNDERSTAND THE NATURE OF THE BEAST

Much opposition is based on false perceptions of what is intended: and, as Tom Peters said to a local government audience in 1988, 'perception is all there is'. Perhaps the heart of the message must be the central rôle that strategic planning plays in achieving change.

DEMONSTRATE DIFFERENCES FROM PAST PRACTICE

This is of particular importance in cases where activities are soured by experiences in the past, for example of corporate planning or structure planning. Strategic planning is not about mounds of paper, legions of inter-departmental working parties, and structures that centralise decision-making. It is about direction, priorities, and change.

INVOLVE COUNCILLORS FROM A VERY EARLY STAGE

This is vital if they are to see strategic planning as helping attain political goals rather than constraining them. But how can councillors best be given the opportunity to debate the sort of issues involved? The committee setting is not always conducive to discussing such matters, particularly across party boundaries. For committee processes are designed for reaching decisions in as business-like a manner as possible, and for formal debate rather than the exploration of ideas in depth.

Cambridgeshire County Council is amongst the authorities best known for their medium-term planning processes; and, from the earliest days, it programmed into the process a cross-party member seminar designed to draw out the major themes that were to be central to the plan. With change in local government having gathered such pace, other authorities have increasingly found it helpful for members to come together outside the committee process to be briefed on — and discuss — major issues affecting strategy. In the space of only one year, for instance, Warwickshire County Council members attended seminars on changing local government finance, compulsory competition, the Education Reform Act, possible changes in the role of social services, community education, and changes to Manpower Services Commission programmes — in all cases, early enough in the process to help shape the Council's response. A similar path has been followed by Surrey County Council; and other authorities are increasingly following suit.

STICK TO THE STRATEGIC

As is explained in Chapter one, if a strategic plan is to be fully effective, it needs to be linked to more detailed programmes of action. But, particularly where the concept of strategic planning is not firmly rooted, it is important that the strategic plan and the action programmes remain distinct. In this way the strategic plan can survive even if circumstances wreak havoc with a particular year's programme of action. Otherwise, if the strategic plan is inseparable from the detail, there is a real danger of fulfilling councillors' fears about inflexibility.

In this particular area, officers have something to learn from election manifestos, many of which are quite explicit at a general level but stop short of commitments at the level of fine detail. Indeed, some manifestos produced before an election end up as the basis of the council's strategy afterwards.

ENSURE THE PLAN IS ROOTED IN PRACTICALITY

This principle is not, in fact, at odds with the previous point. Just as, for most people, it is much easier to think in terms of the concrete rather than the abstract, so policy is easier to get to grips with if it is related to examples. This is the way in which many councillors choose to approach policy issues; and it is a mistake (of which many officers are guilty) to conclude that, just because a discussion is firmly linked to practical examples, it is not about policy. As John Stewart suggests in 'Discussing Policy: Ideas for Improving the Formulation of Policy', many councillors probably think far more strategically than they are normally given credit for.

However, it is important not to confuse illustrating or testing strategic ideas by reference to examples with including tactical details in a strategic plan. The former can be very helpful, and can work against the view that strategic planning is fine in theory but not in practice; the latter can lead to the dreaded path of inflexibility.

EMPHASISE THE IMPORTANCE OF REGULAR REVIEW

This is another vital safeguard against inflexibility. But the key is regular and periodic rather than frequent review. Too frequent reviews will tend to detract from the principle of looking only at the strategic.

DISPEL THE MYTH THAT STRATEGIC PLANNING IS IMPOSSIBLE IN COUNCILS WITHOUT AN OVERALL MAJORITY

An unpublished review of county councils with no majority control carried out in 1986 concluded: 'conventional wisdom suggests that the loss of overall political control makes it nigh on impossible for an authority to plan... The evidence from county councils does not support such a clear conclusion at all'. In fact, some authorities have embarked on a formal planning process only since the loss of an overall majority party.

Nevertheless, there is no denying the fact that particular difficulties for strategic planning can arise in such circumstances. To some extent, though, these can be mitigated in a number of ways.

▽   By focusing on known areas of two-party agreement.
▽   By accepting that some relevant issues may need to be omitted in the interests of gaining at least some agreement.
▽   By trying to ensure that the concept of strategic planning is not adopted jealously by one party as its exclusive idea. In one authority, a gradual move towards strategic planning was set back because the concept of planning was too closely associated with the content of the plan. So, when the plan content secured support from only one party, the concept of planning disappeared with it.
▽   By building in regular reviews from the outset. These may lead to quite significant changes of direction; but at least the authority's officers will know at any one time what direction they are supposed to be going in, and there is less likelihood that different services will be pulling in different directions and working against each other. Changes of direction are infinitely preferable to having no sense of direction at all.

DON'T ADOPT ANOTHER AUTHORITY'S PROCESSES UNCRITICALLY

The circumstances of authorities differ tremendously. And differences are by no means related solely to political complexion. The general principles of strategic planning therefore need to be translated very carefully into customised practices that are going to work in a particular authority. Where there is reluctance to embark on the process, it becomes vital to pay particular heed to the way in which things are traditionally done, so as to jar with the established culture as little as possible. Where there is greater enthusiasm for starting a strategic planning process (e.g. with a change of political control or influx of new councillors), traditional practices may be less relevant — but it is still vital to choose a way forward that people will be comfortable with.

So it is that some authorities have processes that seem to embody good theoretical practice, but which command little interest on the part of councillors; whilst other authorities have more eccentric versions which deliver the goods far more successfully.

BUT DO LEARN FROM OTHER AUTHORITIES' SUCCESSES AND MISTAKES

Whilst the uncritical adoption of what happens elsewhere is usually a grave mistake, there can be obvious advantages in drawing attention to successful practices in authorities held in high regard by one's own. And, more generally, the more one knows about practices elsewhere, the more likely one is to be able to learn from other authorities' successes and mistakes — always provided that there is sensitivity to local circumstances.

DON'T FORGET THAT LABELS CAN HINDER AS WELL AS HELP

Just as adopting conventional forms of strategic planning may not be the best way to command support, so use of the term 'strategic planning' may itself put people off. Where that is the case, change the name. The essence of strategic planning is what it is, not what it is called.

MAKE USE OF ADVICE FROM RESPECTED ORGANISATIONS

The clear exhortations from organisations such as the Audit Commission can be used to good effect in those local authorities where the views of such organisations are influential. But there can be pitfalls. Stories abound of cases where external auditors or consultants have pushed a solution taken straight from the private sector, and have succeeded only in demonstrating their ignorance of political considerations, and reinforcing prejudices against their recommendations!

DON'T START WITH SOMETHING OVER-ELABORATE

One of the mistakes committed by many authorities in the era of corporate planning was the headlong rush into something inappropriately elaborate and sophisticated. At least where enthusiasm for embarking on strategic planning is muted, it may be far better to test the water with something modest, making progress step by step.

The point is well illustrated by F W Ward, a former Town Clerk and Chief Executive of Great Grimsby Borough Council, in an article in 'Local Government Chronicle'. 'The long haul to undertake comprehensive policy planning on such a grand scale proved to be a Herculean task. At times enthusiasm waned ... it was difficult to sustain member interest and involvement ... I think our experience confirmed the view that we had set about the task of programme planning on too ambitious a scale. We had produced documents which were too lengthy and detailed for members to absorb fully.' However, the response of the Authority was not to abandon the process, but rather to simplify it, 'and to focus the Council's attention more upon priorities in the face of an ever-increasing range of needs and problems'.

As well as providing a gradual introduction to a new idea, a modest beginning can have a further advantage: it can help avoid the opposition that might well arise if the introduction of strategic planning required a major investment in resources from the outset, before there was confidence that benefits would result.

TRY TO DEMONSTRATE THE BENEFITS OF STRATEGIC PLANNING AS EARLY AS POSSIBLE

Earlier in this chapter, the point was made that the best way to gain commitment is obviously to show in practice what benefits there are. Clearly, the earlier the achievements of strategic planning emerge, the easier it is to retain commitment.

BUILD THE PRINCIPLES OF STRATEGIC PLANNING INTO MANAGEMENT DEVELOPMENT PROCESSES

The Local Government Training Board publication 'Going for Better Management' makes clear that management development must be firmly rooted in an organisation's own needs. If a local authority is attempting to adopt different ways of working, developing constructive attitudes towards them on the part of managers is as vital a component of management development as is the acquisition of those more traditional skills needed by managers in any organisation. Many authorities have found management development activities to be a highly potent force for change — and for gaining management commitment to change. Without this approach, there is a real danger that officers will fail to see the relevance of strategic planning to them, and will see it as a distraction from their real job of service delivery.

INVOLVE FRONT-LINE DEPARTMENTS

Commitment from front-line departments is harder to obtain — and probably not deserved! — if their involvement is not built into any process from the outset. Strategic planning driven solely from the centre of an organisation may well face an uphill struggle unless the centre is unusually dominant. Moreover, there are many examples of front-line departments embarking upon service strategic planning themselves. Where that is happening, encourage it, build on it, and mould it into the overall strategic planning framework.

DON'T FORGET THE PUBLIC

The initial emphasis may need to be on gaining internal support for the concept of strategic planning within an authority. But, for the reasons set out earlier, there are many advantages in exposing the emerging content of a strategic planning process to public comment. This goes beyond the statutory publishing of strategic land-use proposals in structure and local plans produced under the Town and Country Planning legislation, although authorities' wider strategic plans will of course need to take such development issues carefully into account.

   In 1986, for example, the Royal Borough of Windsor & Maidenhead addressed the issues 'Where We Are — And Where We Are Going' in a free, easily read, 18-page colour brochure, inviting public comments via a form provided (see Fig. 3.1). Coventry City Council produces a free newspaper each year, as part of its annual policy review process, inviting members of the public

The Royal Borough's Strategy Document outlining proposals
for the development of services and facilities

THE ROYAL BOROUGH

YOUR FREE COPY

WayAhead

Our shopping centres
No Entry for the motor
vehicle?

The problems with parking
Solutions with more
imagination

Traditional high streets
How they can survive

Recreation
Planning for more leisure
time

Windsor Castle
Should the tourist help
with our costs?

Maidenhead centre
Time for a town square

Life in the village
Preservation with
prosperity

Royal Borough of Windsor and Maidenhead

Figure 3.1 Way Ahead
Source: Royal Borough of Windsor and Maidenhead 'Way Ahead'

PLANNING FOR THE FUTURE

PLANS FOR the future development of city council services were described by Leader of the Council, Jim Cunningham, as bold and innovative when he unveiled them this week.

Among a whole range of suggestions for improvements to services is a radical new strategy for social services, which maps out how the council will improve its care for disadvantaged people in Coventry.

Also included in the city council's new draft City Policy Guide are proposals for education which address the requirements of the Government's new Education Reform Act.

Other plans for bringing more jobs to the city, city centre redevelopment, leisure services and housing are put forward.

The proposals in the City Policy Guide cover the years 1989 to 1993, and outline how all of the wide range of services provided for Coventry people will be improved.

Councillor Cunningham emphasised that the guide, approved by the council on Tuesday, December 13, was only a draft for consultation.

"Whilst we believe this package represents a bold and innovative response to the challenges facing us over the next few years, we want to hear what the people of Coventry think before going any further," he explained.

Formal consultation with business ratepayers, trades unions and other groups will be taking place over the next four weeks. Comments from individual citizens are also welcome.

A special four-page supplement summarising the detailed proposals is included in this edition of CONTACT. Copies of the City Policy Guide are available for inspection at all Coventry libraries.

You can give us your views by writing to the Customer Relations Unit, Freepost (CV1108), Coventry CV1 5BR. You do not need to use a stamp. Comments must be received by Tuesday, January 10, 1989.

Jim Cunningham, Leader of Coventry City Council

Figure 3.2 Contact
Source: Coventry City Council 'Contact'

to have their say on proposals for the following financial year (see Fig. 3.2). And Thamesdown Borough Council published a short strategy statement in 1985, entitled 'A New Vision for Thamesdown — Strategy Statement', following on from a consultation exercise the previous year.

Achieving support

The process of gaining support for and getting started on strategic planning needs to be therefore both subtle and comprehensive. Most of all it means concentrating on:

▽   involvement — of both members and officers
▽   relevance — being of direct assistance in securing better management and better services
▽   being tailor-made — devising a process that fits comfortably in the individual local authority
▽   simplicity — adopting a strategic planning system that is only as complicated as it really needs to be
▽   showing that real benefits will emerge early.

Review questions

▲   What resistance to strategic planning is evident in your authority?
▲   What opportunities could there be in your authority to encourage political discussion of strategic issues outside the normal committee process?
▲   Do councillors in your authority in fact engage in rather more strategic thinking than they are given credit for?
▲   If your Council has no party with an overall majority of votes, to what extent is the lack of overall political control merely an excuse for not attempting strategic planning?
▲   How good are you at learning from other authorities without adopting their ideas uncritically?
▲   Does management development in your authority help further the cause of strategic planning?

4   Putting the plan together

Key points

▲ Strategic planning is not just about figures and forecasts.
▲ A strategic plan also needs to express vision, values, and directions.
▲ Ideally, it should tackle options, contingencies, and priorities.
▲ It also needs to look beyond the local authority to the community it serves.

Preparing the strategic plan

So far this book has dealt with the background to strategic planning, and the preparatory work that local authorities must put in to embark on it successfully. This chapter is concerned with the basic practicalities of what a strategic plan is likely to look like — the contents.

Looking into the future: the external context

The first basic task of a strategic plan is to try to appreciate and understand how demographic, economic, social, and other trends are shaping, and will shape, the environment in which the local authority operates. Part of that background, of course, is made up of the developing needs, aspirations, and attitudes of local residents and other users of council services.

Perhaps the most comprehensive example of speculating on these changes is Cambridgeshire County Council's 'Ten Year Outlook'. This well-written and well-researched document analyses a range of factors likely to affect the County Council's services.

The main points that the 1987–97 forecasts highlighted were:

▽ **population trends** — picking out particularly:
  — the rapid increase in children aged 10 and under, with consequences for the provision of nursery and primary schools, and child care services
  — the fall in numbers of school leavers, causing labour supply problems for the local economy generally and the County Council specifically
  — a 40% increase by the end of the century in the number of people aged over 80, putting a strain on welfare services.
▽ **transport**
  — increases in road traffic of between 40% and 80% over the next ten years, putting a premium on road-building and road maintenance
  — 20% of households (mainly elderly) still without cars by the year 2000, underlining the continuing need for public transport — a need that is

further reinforced by even more households not having access to a car
during the day.

▽ **social trends**
— a background of increasing crime, particularly criminal damage, auto
crime, and offences against the person
— a 40% increase over the next 10 years in elderly single-person
households, arguing for more investment in sheltered or very sheltered
housing schemes and domiciliary support services
— more single parent families, reinforcing demands on child-care and
childminding services.

But dipping into the future means more than projecting statistical trends.
It also entails some informed speculative thinking. For example,
Cambridgeshire's 'Ten Year Outlook' also examined:

▽ the prospects and consequences of increased personal leisure time
▽ the implications of heightened activity by voluntary organisations and
pressure groups, attempting to influence public attitudes and local
authority action
▽ the impact of developments in information technology on education,
working practices, and recruitment.

In a similar set of statistical analyses, Arun District Council explored the
continuing trend of bulk shopping moving out of traditional town centres to
peripheral sites. Suffolk County Council examined differing geographical
trends, sharpened by the buoyancy of the local economy along the A45
corridor.

There are many other examples throughout local government. This
cannot be surprising because statistical forecasts and informed speculation are
essential building blocks for any attempts at formulating policy. A strategic
plan covering a council's activities as a whole must be underpinned by analysis
of changes that it must, or may well have to, cope with.

Yet — to repeat a point that crops up again and again in this book, since it
is at the core of the topic — it is vital that such analyses and speculations are
kept selective in a corporate process. Obviously, authorities differ in the
degree to which there is an appetite for detail on the part of councillors and
senior managers. But the lessons of the past all point to the danger that
excessive length or detail will lead to loss of interest. And even where interest is
not lost, effectiveness often is: there are only so many issues that an
organisation can address strategically without dissipating its effort.

Looking into the future: the internal response

Local government is a creature of statute. What local authorities do is
therefore constrained, shaped, directed, and circumscribed by the legal
framework that Parliament and central government set. The implications of
recent legislation were set out in Chapter one; but an effective strategic plan
must not only explore the general consequences of recent legislation but also
develop some feel for the direction of future legislation. The purpose is not to
examine what services the council might or might not be responsible for in
coming years. Rather it is to gain some insight into how the authority needs to

develop as an organisation in order to be really effective within the legal framework which the Government sets.

Chapter one depicted the emerging role of the local authority as a result of legislative change as:

▽   the securer but not necessarily the provider of services
▽   the enabler or facilitator — helping to make things happen
▽   the quality controller of services provided by others.

This new picture is rapidly acquiring the status of conventional wisdom, encouraged not least by the publication of a pamphlet entitled 'The Local Right — enabling not providing' by the current Secretary of State for the Environment, albeit writing in a private capacity. But it is one thing for a concept to gain currency: it is quite another for it to be translated into action. And it is here that strategy is so important. For a strategic plan is a proper vehicle for addressing not just what services are to be provided, but also:

▽   who is to provide those services
▽   how they are to be provided (if by the local authority)
▽   what major changes are needed within the local authority to ensure their provision.

Berkshire County Council dealt with this issue in its 'Medium Term Planning 1989–92'. It confronted the issue of how to tackle a future where 'it is no longer sensible to assume:

▽   that service spending will increase from year to year
▽   that authorities exist to provide more services in quantitative terms
▽   that direct provision by the Council is the best way of meeting needs'.

Its response was to change the focus of the organisation 'from the centre to the services provided and beyond them to all who come into contact with the Authority, be they clients, ratepayers, residents, businesses or visitors'.

This emphasis on what is variously termed decentralised resource management, managerial devolution, or delegated management is being echoed by more and more authorities, as they see the need to push responsibility out and down, in the interests of:

▽   meeting customer needs better
▽   avoiding bureaucratic delays
▽   job enrichment for cost centre and other sharp-end managers
▽   freeing senior managers to act strategically.

Such a trend, combined with the organisational implications of compulsory competitive tendering, has prompted considerable thought about changing roles and relationships within local authorities. No longer are the workings of an authority best portrayed by a diagram that emphasises departmental boundaries (see Fig. 4.1). For sharply differentiated roles are emerging *within* individual services, well summed up by consultants Kinsley Lord in a report ('Cambridgeshire County Council Into the 1990s') in 1989:

▽   **strategic buyers** — these carry out a strategic role, in which client needs are identified, given priority within the political framework and then matched with the resources available in order to determine requirements

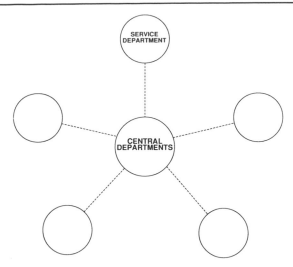

Figure 4.1 Conventional Departmental Structure

▽ **service brokers** — acting as agents for the strategic buyers, these take the
   strategic requirements and convert them into technical specifications in
   contracts, then contract the services with potential service providers (both
   internally and externally). They also monitor the performance of the
   service providers on behalf of the strategic buyers.
▽ **service providers** — these perform an operational rôle, providing services
   direct to clients to meet contractual specifications as to volume, quality,
   cost, and time.

The model can be taken further. Providers in one service have much in
common with another; and so it is that a number of authorities are already
going down the track of grouping together their in-house contractors (the
direct service organisations under the Local Government Act of 1988),
sometimes in a free-standing department. At the other end of the chain, the
strategic functions of different services have a lot in common with each other
— and with the really strategic 'strategic buyers' at the centre of the
organisation. Although departmental boundaries tend to persist in this area,
one can expect to see strengthened linkages in the future.

The overall result may be an authority whose functional organisation is
better represented by Fig. 4.2 than 4.1. It may seem that the organisation is
breaking apart. If schools opt out of local authority control, or business units
go down the path of management buy-outs, there will clearly be some truth in
the notion. And even without such outcomes, there is no denying the
distancing of service and business units from the core. But equally significant
may be the greater cohesion of the core itself — certainly an aid to strategic
management.

Another area of change is the relationship between support services and
the rest of the organisation. As a result of:

▽ the commercial pressures bearing on direct labour and direct service
   organisations

▽   the imminent arrival of greater managerial freedom for many schools and colleges
▽   similar changes for other managers under decentralised resource management
▽   the sheer pressure of ever tighter financial resources.

customer-based support services are finding themselves increasingly having commercial and quasi-commercial pressures passed on to them. The result is a move towards a more tightly defined semi-contractual relationship in which attempts are made to agree service quality, quantity, and price in advance, and in which payment is more direct than the traditional end-of-year recharge beyond the control of the customer department.

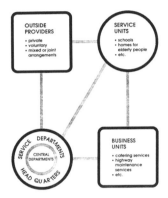

Figure 4.2 Changing Organisation Structure

Such matters may seem a long way from the traditional local authority planning document. However, they represent ways in which councils are attempting to put themselves in a position to confront the external challenges facing them; and it is hard to see how a strategic plan can square up to the challenges without tackling the internal issues as well.

Nor is it merely that changing functions and relationships are proper matters for inclusion in a strategic plan. It is also the case that the particular changes involved actually increase the need for strategic planning. For the new order sketched here puts much greater emphasis than in the past on arms-length management. When one has day-to-day control over all elements of a process, one can attempt (whatever the cost to efficiency or effectiveness) to muddle through without a strategy. But this becomes nigh on impossible when much of the process lies in the hands of agencies that are partly or wholly independent, and which operate according to pre-arranged contracts.

Finding out

A strategic plan must not be solely an inward-looking document, reflecting the pressures and perceptions of local government councillors and officers. It must also be grounded in the real problems and concerns felt by local residents, businesses, and the customers of the council's services.

This principle has long been acknowledged in town and country planning, where there has been considerable emphasis on public participation in plan preparation for two decades. But in many other services the persistence of a professional culture has meant that decisions about what people need have all too frequently paid scant regard to what the community and individual clients actually think. It has taken the recent spread of a customer service culture to prompt more general interest in gauging public opinion in some services; and the same is broadly true of authority-wide plans.

However, there have been notable exceptions. Mention is made in Chapter three of some authorities that invite public comment on authority-wide plans; and, in the field of market research, the London Borough of Richmond-upon-Thames has contracted MORI to sample residents' opinions annually since 1984. The findings inform, and feed into, the annual planning process. For example, tenants' dissatisfaction with housing identified by the survey has been reduced significantly through a policy of increased emphasis on customer service.

There have recently been many more examples of market research surveys of particular services and for local authorities as a whole. The test of their effectiveness will be how far finding out translates into proposals for action as part of the strategic planning process.

Injecting values

A strategic plan should not be just a cold statistical report. Moreover, it is not just about anticipating trends. It also needs to strike right at the heart of influencing the culture and ethos of the organisation. That means building on the fundamental principles that guide the local authority's behaviour.

Cheshire County Council has captured this theme succinctly in its Mission Statement.

▽   The purpose of the Council is to serve the Cheshire people.
▽   Councillors and employees are accountable to the Cheshire people.
▽   The County Council will act with honesty, integrity, and respect for the individual in its dealings with the public.
▽   The County Council is a partnership between councillors and employees.
▽   The County Council's most important resource is its employees.

Wrekin District Council has articulated in a simple way the values that the Council wishes to espouse. They are quality, caring, and fairness, and are summed up in the phrase 'Being the Best'. Wansdyke District Council has encapsulated its basic values in the words 'Service is our business', and Braintree District Council in 'Braintree Means Business'. In Gloucestershire County Council, agreement on a statement of organisational culture followed wide consultation among employees and councillors. The outcome was 'Gloucestershire — at your service'.

Values are not neutral statements. They describe the philosophy of the council. Because they do that, at the very least they must reflect political aspirations, even if the nature of the council means that those are pragmatic rather than dogmatic.

Giving a sense of direction

Strategic planning means giving the local authority a sense of direction and practical purpose. Of course, that also means political direction and purpose in the sense that the strategic plan must express the council's view on its future role and organisation.

The London Borough of Richmond upon Thames prefaced its 'Operational Plan 1988/89–1989/90' with a very clear statement of the Council's purpose:

> This is an articulate community with high expectations and aspirations. It requires high quality public services closely attuned to the wishes of residents. The Council has adopted a people-orientated philosophy of customer care, public service and public accountability. This sense of purpose underlies our emphasis on public consultation, involving local people in decisions which are likely to affect them; our opening of all formal meetings to the public and our readiness to involve the public in Council affairs. It underlies our emphasis on market research, actively and systematically seeking the views of the public as service users and customers, about the Council as a whole and about particular services. It reflects our readiness to work in partnership with parents as school governors and members of the Education Committee and to hold regular local area consultation meetings where committee chairmen and Ward members can be called to account. It is reflected in our Area Housing Management Committees involving tenants in the management of council estates and in our decentralised approach to service provision. At management level accountability is emphasised by the Annual Reports on each service area, setting targets for future achievement and reviewing performance, particularly in the light of customer views. It also underlies our wish to involve staff at all levels more closely in the development of the services and the improvement of the organisation.
>
> The adoption in practice of this philosophy at all levels is proving to be a major element in improving the Council's performance and fitting the style and contents of its services to the needs and wishes of Borough residents. It is contributing to the basic philosophy behind individual service strategies. But it is not a straight forward matter to apply these concepts in practice throughout the organisation. They contrast with traditional ways in local government. Time and consistent effort are required. A people-orientated approach to management does not come cheaply but it will be money well spent if a quality service is to be achieved.

Bradford City Council was equally forthright in spelling out where it saw itself going, when it launched its Social Strategy in 1987. 'The Council has only one strategy — the Social Strategy which encompasses all other issues that the Council faces.' To Bradford the Social Strategy meant:

▽ putting people first
▽ decentralisation of operational management
▽ client orientation
▽ co-operative working
▽ assertive local government.

The change in political control in 1988 brought a very different but no less clear sense of direction.

Northamptonshire County Council set down the philosophy and seven principles which would guide its decisions and actions during the Council's term of office from 1985–89. The general philosophy was that 'the community is best served by an efficient, well run authority, providing good quality and effective services in response to a clear picture of need'.

The seven principles that underpinned that philosophy were:

∇   policy on rate levels and income from fees and charges
∇   business management
∇   support to communities, families, and voluntary organisations
∇   choice of service
∇   employee pride and standards of service
∇   alternative service provision
∇   the environment.

The recurrent theme is to take the local authority in a particular direction. That must be the fundamental purpose underlying any strategic planning document.

A selective focus

John Stewart said in his publication 'Strategic Management in Local Government' that 'a strategy that is concerned with everything is concerned with nothing — for it has failed to separate out the strategic'. The test of an effective strategic plan is the extent to which it focuses successfully on:

∇   issues that confront the authority as a whole
∇   issues that present themselves in several parts of the authority, but are best tackled coherently
∇   issues that are confined to a single service but are of such magnitude that dealing with them inevitably impacts elsewhere.

The 'Gloucestershire Review 1988' identified 13 major issues that it had to tackle over the following few years. They illustrate all three types of issue, and are set out on pages 38–39.

In a similar way, in its 'Medium Term Planning 1989–92', Berkshire County Council picked out just four key management issues:

∇   devolved management
∇   competitive tendering
∇   recruitment and retention of employees
∇   the importance of investment in information technology to the development of services.

Arun District Council in its 'Strategy Papers and Programme Plans 1987–91' identified what it termed five essential components of its strategy — somewhere between key issues and outline solutions:

∇   a much improved awareness of the community's profile and potential needs with public services viewed in terms of user benefits not product features
∇   a greater understanding of the Council's legitimate involvement with other

public sector organisations leading to a Member focus on significant issues
and an organisational capacity for the exercise of influence

▽   a corporate image presentation that stresses the attractiveness of the
District in its ability to support a well balanced life-style, and the quality
and warmth of the Authority in caring for its customers

▽   a hierarchical approach to the provision of services both within and
between the programme areas covering:

    (a)   statutory and other essential services required to facilitate the
community and individuals therein leading their own lives in a
beneficial and independent manner

    (b)   additional support services directed towards the disadvantaged
minorities in the community

    (c)   further discretionary services materially shaped by consumer choice
and filling a particular niche in the competitive market place

with the selected relative priority areas being Community Care Services,
Public Services, and Strategic/Economic Development Services

▽   a responsible employer position that acknowledges the vital place of 'core'
staff in sustaining its purposes and the necessity of developing progressive
personnel policies as the base for mutual achievement and satisfaction.

These examples all serve to illustrate the crucial point that effective
strategic planning means selective strategic planning.

Options, contingencies, and priorities

Three basic elements in the classic planning process are:

▽   exploring different ways of tackling problems and issues — i.e. options
▽   working out how to cope with alternative eventualities — i.e.
contingencies
▽   distilling the key tasks and policies within resource constraints and other
limitations — i.e. priorities.

The first two are steps that published strategic plans in local government
are noticeably shy and reticent about, although commendable progress has
been made in a number of authorities with making a stand over priorities.

OPTIONS

The fairly broad statements of policy that emerge in strategic plans evolve out
of political debate, often entailing widespread consultation and discussion
between councillors, officers, and the community. The emergence of policy is
therefore a subtle process, with the range of options through which discussion
has progressed rarely able to be captured in any explicit way. At the level of
authority-wide plans, those options that are discussed are rarely revealed.

    Furthermore, the agenda that strategic planning is tackling now is one
dominated largely by fairly common demographic and social trends, and
national legislative changes. The scope for manoeuvre is therefore somewhat
constrained. Nevertheless, even within the context of the move towards
'enabling' at the expense of direct service provision, there is room for choice,

(1) **The effects of development throughout the county**

The increasing buoyancy of the economy brings with it major costs in providing, on very short time-scales, the necessary infrastructure to support concentrated development. New services and facilities, including more extensive highways networks, are a drain on already limited resources. Trying to maintain existing assets and re-allocation between rural, urban, and development areas is creating difficult choices for the authority.

Major impact on:
Provision of Infrastructure
Maintenance and Management of Assets
Maintenance of Services to the Rural Areas
Secondary Reorganisation

(2) **The growth in the 75+ client group**

The rise of nearly 3,100 in the number of pensioners coupled with an increase of 16% for the over 80s in the period 1988–93 will potentially have a dramatic effect in a number of areas for which this group are clients.

Major impact on:
Social Services Care of the Elderly
Public Transport

(3) **Persistent high unemployment in specific areas**

Whilst Gloucestershire as a whole fares relatively well in employment terms, there are still problems in specific areas and with specific types (e.g. long term) of unemployment which need continued and concerted attention.

Major impact on:
Economic Development
Training for Jobs
Tourism

(4) **The rise in the level of reported crime**

The increase in the level of crime in the county, and in the country generally, highlights the role and contribution of the Council and its associated services in preventing, or at least minimising, the opportunities for crime.

Major impact on:
Crime Prevention initiatives by all departments
Security of Buildings
Youth and Community Work
Probation

(5) **Competitive tendering**

The Council must prepare for the challenge presented by the extension of competitive tendering, ensuring wherever possible that its services are equipped to compete.

Major impact on:
Grounds Maintenance
Vehicle Maintenance
Maintenance of Roads
Catering
Cleaning
Central Services

(6) **The role of the Local Education Authority**

The traditional responsibilities of the Local Education Authority are being eroded and Gloucestershire must continue to take steps to alter its present approach and practices in response to changed circumstances.

Major impact on:
Education Service

(7) **The Community Charge**

The significance of the introduction of the Community Charge lies in the potential effect it will have on the resources available to the authority and in the change in attitude towards budgeting necessary for both members and officers. Inevitably, there will also be a change in relationship with the public.

Major impact on:
Members
Budgeting Arrangements
Public Relations

(8) **The responsibilities imposed by recent social services legislation**

Recent legislation in the Social Services field has resulted in significantly increased responsibilities in care in the community and work with the disabled without providing the necessary level of increased resources. National focus on such areas as child sexual abuse has also caused extra demands to be made on the service. If the County Council is to meet these demands it may need to reassess its priorities.

Major impact on:
Social Services

(9) **The need to reassess methods of service delivery**

It can no longer be assumed that any service should necessarily be provided directly by the local authority. Legislation may require that it be put out to tender; local knowledge may dictate that voluntary organisations should be involved; management style may conclude that there are new and more innovative styles of delivery. The aim must be to provide the best service in the best way possible.

Major impact on:
Service Reviews
Partnership with Voluntary Organisations
Equal Opportunities
Management Development

(10) **Change in the countryside**

A variety of forces are at work in the more rural areas of the county. Some are facing development and tourism pressures, others are threatened by changes in the agricultural industry, in many the continued provision of services by both the private and public sectors remains uncertain and in virtually all, local residents face problems in finding low cost housing.

Major impact on:
Planning
Rural Services

(11) **Waste disposal**

Due to the economic upsurge increased input to county tips of both domestic and industrial waste has considerably shortened their anticipated life with a resultant need to search for alternative facilities as a matter of urgency.

Major impact on:
Waste Disposal

(12) **Post-16 education**

Developments in the funding of higher colleges are necessitating radical changes in the way that post-16 education is provided in the county. Swift and decisive action needs to be taken to protect the future of higher education and of GlosCAT.

Major impact on:
Education

(13) **Provision for the under fives**

In view of the importance attached by the County Council to its Equal Opportunities Policy and the noted increase in single parent families, all steps should be taken to maintain the improvement in pre-school provision.

Major impact on:
Education
Social Services.

from: *Gloucestershire Review 1988*

and therefore for the definition of options. At one extreme is the much-quoted example of the U.S. council that supposedly meets once a year over lunch to award the contracts. (If its affairs were wholly governed by the 1988 Local Government Act, it would of course not have to meet so frequently!) At the other extreme is the type of authority that is set against contemplating any dilution in its traditional direct service provision rôle. Most lie somewhere in between, and it is a broad spectrum.

What is particularly interesting is the way the current agenda is drawing out pragmatic responses that blur the stereotyped party-political differences.

▽ One authority where the Labour group holds all committee chairs has allowed the transfer to the private sector of data processing and building design. There were compelling operational reasons; and careful safeguards were written into the contracts. But it was done without legislative compulsion; and the fact remains that few Conservative-led councils have gone so far down that particular path.

▽ By contrast, the chief officers of a firmly Conservative-controlled authority tackled the council leader head-on with the question of how much the politicians really wanted to beat the private sector in competitive tendering. The strong, positive answer left them in no doubt that councillors put pride in the organisation for which they were responsible before any ideological views about the size of the public sector.

Warwickshire County Council's document 'The Challenges Ahead' canvasses six possible future roles for the County Council over the succeeding four to five years:

▽ direct service provider
▽ regulator and quality controller
▽ enabler and co-ordinator
▽ contractor
▽ entrepreneur
▽ partner.

Whilst it stops short of presenting them as options, it does underline that the choice is one of emphasis rather than total adoption or rejection. And it acknowledges that attitudes to emerging roles may differ from service to service: 'members may be happy for the County Council to be a provider of last resort where industrial estates are concerned; they may — reluctantly or otherwise — acknowledge the role of the private and voluntary sectors in residential care; but would they want to see the County Council's education function shrivel to that of a safety net?'

As confidence in strategic planning develops within local government, it may be that making options more explicit will prove more feasible. Greater involvement of the public may encourage it.

CONTINGENCIES

Given that reactive administration has held sway over strategic management throughout much of local government, it is hardly surprising if going the whole hog and producing not just a strategic plan but a series of strategic contingency plans has not yet caught on. It may even be tempting to dismiss the concept in the late 1980s as unnecessary in the face of what seem to be unmistakably clear external pressures. But the 1990s are a mistier prospect altogether; and inflexible plans run the risk of repeating one of the mistakes of the corporate planning era. Here is an area crying out for some trail-blazing work.

PRIORITIES

Choosing between different services in a multi-purpose authority is an unenviable task. How does one set about assessing the relative priorities of extinguishing fires, housing the homeless, and helping frail elderly people — even if armed with a clear political philosophy? But continuing pressure on resources must inevitably put priority choices increasingly in the spotlight. And even if explicit priority choices are ducked, choices will effectively emerge anyway: for instance, the implicit choice to give priority to the status quo, or to yesterday's crisis.

To local government's credit, priorities for shorter-term action are both common and clear cut, spelling out both:

▽   what is to be done
▽   how resources are to be allocated.

But priorities are vital for longer-term plans also. A strategy can survive without options — if democratic pressures allow it. It may also survive without contingencies — despite living dangerously. But a strategic plan that fails to address priorities is a negation of strategic thought — which means focusing on selectivity.

Reaching out into the community

Increasingly, local government is becoming less involved in doing, and more involved in influencing and helping to do. The strategic plan therefore is not simply about shaping the narrower range of activities in which the council itself is involved, but also about reaching out beyond its own organisation. It needs to set a strategy that engages other agencies, and the community, with the aim of stimulating constructive co-operation to improve the overall quality of life.

'A New Vision for Thamesdown — A Consultation Document 1984' (Thamesdown Borough Council), produced in 1985, illustrates this well. It developed the theme 'in which leadership, encouragement, and support replace direct and all-embracing large-scale control'. The strategy examined the scope for direction and influence through:

▽   ownership of land and property — recognising that partnership in development goes only some way to securing what Thamesdown wants, and is also dependent on inputs from other agencies
▽   services — reaffirming the move from mandatory services to the provision of discretionary services aimed at maintaining and improving the area's attractiveness and quality of life
▽   planning — with reducing direct control over development, the implementation of objectives involving private sector land use and high environmental standards relies much more on a strong planning role

▽   advocacy — identifying the essential need to build up an advocacy role in order to gain the trust and confidence of other service agencies, the government, business, and the general public in furthering Thamesdown's aims.

But it is not just the growth of the enabling role that makes it important to have a strategy that reaches out beyond the authority itself. The importance also lies in the opportunity provided to engage wider community support, to blur the distinction between council and locality, and to encourage the return of the view that the local authority is the natural focus of community aspirations — rather than just the agency responsible for a few specific services.

The main elements of a strategic plan

In summary, therefore, a strategic plan is likely to include:

▽   forecasts of population, social, and other trends
▽   consideration of the authority's organisational response to these
▽   analysis of customer attitudes and aspirations
▽   the expression of underlying values and sense of direction that are bound to reflect political thinking
▽   an examination of the options, contingencies, and priorities for the development of the local authority and its services
▽   looking beyond the local authority to the community it serves.

Review questions

▲   How good is your authority at concentrating on a limited number of selected issues?
▲   Are there proposals to change internal relationships in response to changing roles?
▲   How much emphasis is put on customer attitudes in deciding on future courses of action?
▲   Does your authority have a clearly understood set of values, and a clear sense of direction?
▲   How much thought is given to options, contingencies, and priorities?
▲   Do any authority-wide plans look beyond the activities of the authority itself?

5 Getting started and keeping going

Key points

▲ The stimulus for strategic planning can come from a variety of sources.
▲ And responsibility for keeping it going can be vested in different parts of the organisation.
▲ But the key to success is harnessing the involvement of as many parts as possible.

Getting started

It is possible to be prescriptive to a degree in listing the contents of a strategic plan. That cannot be so in describing how to go about preparing one. The only certainties are that strategic planning will do best where:

▽ it helps politicians and officers both to address and to solve their problems
▽ politicians and officers are involved thoroughly in the process so that the resulting strategic plan is of value to both categories.

To get started on strategic planning means sparking enthusiasm and belief that it is both relevant and essential to managing the council better. That spark can come from a variety of sources.

COUNCILLORS

As is mentioned in Chapter 2, strong political direction emerged in Arun District Council in the early 1980s, and a new Chief Executive was appointed in 1983 with the specific remit to manage under political direction. The brief was to move the authority from one working on traditional lines to one that ran its affairs in a business-like way, and took on its wider responsibilities for community well-being. Crucial to the implementation of this political imperative was the development of a strategic plan.

Similarly, in Wansdyke District Council, strong political leadership not only prompted radical changes in management organisation, but also set an agenda for change in which of necessity strategic planning and thinking had to play important roles.

These are two encouraging examples of councillors realising the value of, and need for, a strategic approach. It has to be said that, in all too many authorities, councillors lack an appetite for strategic thought, but are happy to involve themselves in more detailed matters.

One note of caution needs to be sounded. Few officers fall into the trap of seeing councillors as a homogeneous group, and of believing that all will be equally enthusiastic for a particular initiative. But the assumption is often made that the only divide is along party lines — and this assumption ignores the reality of the different viewpoints held by leading councillors on the one hand and 'backbenchers' on the other. Even — or perhaps especially? — in authorities without a majority party, there can be that sort of polarisation across party boundaries. Just as senior officers must not lose sight of the need to carry their more junior colleagues with them, so those with an interest in promoting strategic planning need to remain alive to the danger of leading member support existing in the absence of wider member interest.

SENIOR MANAGEMENT

More common are authorities where the drive for strategic planning comes from officers. In Gloucestershire County Council, for instance, the main stimulus for change in the late 1980s came from the Chief Executive and his senior managers. The theme that has driven forward strategic planning in the Council has been value for money, with committees having 'a small number of key tasks for the year ahead focusing members' and officers' attention on those areas where we want to make real progress'.

Similarly, in Braintree District Council, it is from top officers that commitment has come to the introduction of strategic planning. Its medium-term strategy — 'The Way Forward' — was formulated largely by the Chief Executive and colleague chief and second-tier officers servicing a members' working group.

EXTERNAL PROMPTINGS

But it is not always from internal sources that the drive comes. The major changes in the strategic management of Cheshire County Council from 1988 followed a report from consultants. Admittedly, it was the authority that initiated the overall review of management arrangements; but it was the findings of the consultants' review that pointed the way to the changes subsequently undertaken.

Similarly, in the mid 1980s, Northumberland County Council asked the Audit Commission to undertake a value-for-money review of its services and management arrangements. One of the outcomes of that study was the suggestion that the Council should adopt a more systematic and strategic approach to the planning and management of services, a suggestion that has since been taken up.

A FOCUS ON PERFORMANCE REVIEW

Avon County Council began to address strategic planning in 1986 when it introduced the concept of performance review on a comprehensive basis. The focus of attention on standards of service and performance that such activity prompted led rapidly to a systematic approach to strategic planning.

BUILDING ON MEDIUM-TERM FINANCIAL PLANNING

For a number of years Cambridgeshire County Council has prepared rolling three-year medium-term plans, linked to a one-year financial budget. The medium-term plans have a substantial financial emphasis, but also embrace setting objectives for services and evaluating performance. The grounding in this exercise and the experience gained from it are now leading naturally into developing a 'corporate strategy' — focusing political attention on the major issues ahead.

THE AMALGAMATION OF SERVICE PLANS

Some authorities have individual services that display strategic management, but without it existing at the authority-wide level. Others — such as the London Borough of Southwark — have derived strategic priorities for the council as a whole by taking as their starting point individual services' priorities. Yet others — such as Northumberland County Council — have taken a conscious, corporate decision to start with service issues and only to build up into an authority-wide plan at a later stage.

If, in such circumstances, the resulting authority-wide plan is little more than the sum of the service plans, it is not likely to be very effective as a strategy, for two reasons. Firstly, it is unlikely to be able to get to grips with inter-service priorities, especially in resource allocation. And, secondly, it is unlikely to be effective at tackling those issues — of increasing importance — that cut across service boundaries.

On the other hand, taking service plans as a starting point can be a useful way of winning the commitment of those who would resent the imposition of a 'central' viewpoint seen as remote from the real world of service delivery. In practice, the process is usually a combined one, since a strategy that ignores service realities is likely to be as ineffective as one that fails to draw out common threads.

An interesting example is provided by Berkshire County Council, which has developed both a top-down and bottom-up approach to the planning of services. It has a scene-setting medium-term plan at the top, whilst at the bottom it has identified approximately 700 cost centres (excluding schools and colleges), each with a business plan showing budgets, staffing, key targets, performance indicators, and outline emerging issues. Each influences the other.

Keeping going

Sustaining the momentum of strategic planning is at least as difficult as getting started. There is no one model of success.

In some authorities the lead is taken by central policy, planning, or research units. For example, in Wrekin District Council the Policy Unit is central to much of the strategic planning activity. In Wiltshire County Council, a small Policy Planning Unit was established in January 1988 to co-ordinate the introduction of policy planning. There are many other such examples. The strength of this approach is that it ensures that:

▽   the right skills are available to undertake the strategic planning work
▽   there are people with both time and enthusiasm for the task.

On the other hand, relying upon a central unit brings the risks of:

▽   marginalising strategic planning — making it 'their' job and not
     collectively 'ours'
▽   divorcing it from the mainstream of council activity and therefore making
     it less likely to be relevant and central to the better management of services
▽   reinforcing the suspicion that strategy and policy is only for 'the centre',
     and not for those who manage and deliver services.

For the central unit to be sure of avoiding these pitfalls, therefore, careful
thought needs to be given before it goes beyond:

▽   preparing
▽   informing
▽   stimulating
▽   facilitating
▽   assisting
▽   co-ordinating
▽   monitoring progress.

Commitment and involvement must spread deeply and widely throughout
the organisation, in one way or another.

Some authorities have kept central involvement to a minimum, relying
more on inter-departmental teams to develop and maintain strategic planning.
For example, Warwickshire County Council's approach has been to use a
senior manager from a service department to work with and through mainly
deputy chief officers on the early stages of strategic planning, albeit under firm
direction from the Chief Executive and Assistant Chief Executive. This group
responsibility is similar to that adopted in Braintree District Council.

The advantages are that this approach:

▽   spreads responsibility for strategic planning through the organisation and
     is more likely to engender collective commitment and enthusiasm
▽   draws on knowledge and skills across departments, and emphasises the
     shared ownership of the strategic plan.

The clearly apparent drawbacks are the risks of:

▽   lack of momentum, and low motivation unless there is a well structured,
     receptive environment in which strategic planning is encouraged to thrive
▽   lack of continuity as staff turnover dilutes both knowledge and
     commitment.

This approach is therefore likely to prove most successful where there
exists:

▽   a planning culture
▽   a strategic philosophy
▽   receptiveness to change.

Paradoxically, however, the approach is also a potentially valuable means
of nurturing such characteristics.

Involvement and ownership

A strategic plan is only effective as a tool for achieving change if there is general conviction among both members and officers that it represents a view of the future that reflects both political and managerial problems and aspirations. That ownership and commitment has to be earned by real involvement. That means the involvement of:

▽   elected members
▽   the chief executive and chief officers
▽   other officers who are part of delivering the strategy.

Unless that is achieved, strategic planning can become at best an intellectually satisfying charade because of one or more of the following fatal flaws:

▽   it will not articulate and reflect members' aspirations, and will therefore inspire hostility as an officer document
▽   it will be sidelined by the chief executive and chief officers as a process which informs, but whose relevance is merely to assist in the continuing pattern of reactive crisis management
▽   it will not carry conviction with managers who will fail to see how it helps and supports the immediate task of better service delivery.

Review questions

▲   Where does the greatest impetus for strategic planning lie in your authority?
▲   How can the active involvement of other parts of the organisation be secured?

6 Translating strategy into action

Key points

▲ The purpose behind strategic planning is to help anticipate and guide change.
▲ But change will not be secured simply by the preparation of a strategic plan.
▲ A strategic plan must be underpinned by arrangements that support its implementation.
▲ Complementary management and organisation structures and processes are essential.
▲ So is a supportive management culture, the key to which is management development.

Progressing beyond the strategy

The preparation of a strategic plan is not an end in itself. It is an essential element in guiding the direction and pace of change in a local authority. Alone, however, it will achieve little. It must be part of a framework of overall political, managerial, and organisational arrangements that focus on translating strategy into action. That means underpinning the strategic plan with supportive:

▽ structures, both managerial and political
▽ processes and practices
▽ culture, founded on management and personnel development.

These must all be geared to assist the implementation of strategic objectives.

John Stewart makes the point in his discussion paper 'Strategic Management in Local Government' that 'strategic change could almost be defined as change requiring significant organisational development. Strategic change is about changes that cannot be handled by the present organisation.' This point is reflected in the view put forward in Chapter four of this book that strategic organisational change is itself a proper matter for inclusion in a strategic plan.

But regardless of what a plan actually contains, it is certainly the case that particular organisational responses are needed to support its implementation. It is therefore encouraging that there are growing numbers of local authorities that are matching their decisions on strategy with decisions about management organisation.

Supportive structures

One notable recent example of an authority making structural changes is Cheshire County Council. The stimulus behind its far-reaching departmental reorganisation was its intent to 'make the necessary links between structure and style'. The restructuring was based on six principles:

▽ changes in organisation should create the capacity to achieve effective strategic direction
▽ the Chief Executive is accountable for strategic direction within the objectives and strategies set by members
▽ the Chief Executive is responsible for ensuring that the Council's overall management effort is directed with a sense of common purpose
▽ the Management Board (of Directors) is accountable collectively for planning policy and resource use, for managing the implementation of decisions, for overall performance and for effective communications and relationships both internally and externally
▽ all County Council services should be brought within the purview of the Board
▽ Board members should have individual accountability to the Chief Executive and the Board for strategic management.

As a result, the new management organisation was shaped so that:

▽ there were no departments with conventional chief officers and deputy chief officers
▽ existing services and activities were grouped together in 'directorates' under a Director
▽ there were six service groupings — education, environment, information and leisure, social services, finance & management, and support services, plus the fire service and police service
▽ each Director had a seat on the Management Board, chaired by the Chief Executive
▽ Directors were responsible for policy development and co-ordination, resource management, performance review, and political management
▽ principal services within directorates had service heads responsible for day-to-day management, and focusing on quality and delivery of services
▽ each directorate had its own centralised core support services — embracing administration, personnel, and finance — for all services within the directorate.

Arun District Council recently reorganised its departments on the basis of very similar principles. Its objective was to 'demonstrate a slim market-directed structure supporting public and political needs, and not professional assumptions'.

Wansdyke District Council also transformed a traditional management structure to equip itself better to face the strategic management challenges that it had defined. The former departmental organisation based on a Chief Executive and five chief officers, each heading separate departments, has now been developed into an organisation that draws a clear and sharp distinction between 'support' services and 'direct' services, although both are provided only on a competitive basis. The new structure has a District General Manager, who exercises executive responsibility over all employees through two general managers.

Other local authorities have embarked on less comprehensive management changes. Nevertheless, many are targeted at underpinning strategic direction and decisions. For instance, Kent County Council has radically altered the management structure of its Education department. The balance has shifted from headquarters to area offices, in anticipation of the powerful message of devolved management implicit in the Education Reform Act.

Other local authorities are pioneering different changes in management structure, aimed at giving the organisation new insight, new directions, or new ways of doing things.

The member lead

Changes in management structure will themselves be successful only if they are matched by effective political and member organisation. That means examining the working of committees, working parties, and other member bodies against the same criteria used to test the officer structure:

▽   the recognition of differentiated roles
▽   the presence of clear lines of responsibility and accountability
▽   short decision routes
▽   maximum delegation.

Significantly, those authorities that have carefully examined their officer structures are also prominent amongst those who have reviewed, or are reviewing, the complementary member organisation.

Cheshire County Council took forward changes in its officer and member structure broadly at the same time. It identified three main roles for members, each of which demanded a different form of structure:

▽   **policy development** — where committees are too formal and restrictive for developing policies. Instead, the Council is developing the concept of member panels, and proposing a range of these across all committees.
▽   **general management** — with the emphasis on formal processes and decision-taking to which the committee system lends itself.
▽   **local representation and external relationships** — which is the role of members as individuals, and despite being concerned with service delivery and customer relations is where performance is now most variable. Improvement is seen as coming through better member support services, and through focusing on the importance of the rôle and on the way in which the Council is perceived by its electors and its public image is formed.

Arun District Council also forged developments in parallel in its political and officer organisation. These have ensured member leadership and management of strategic policies through:

▽ a strong Policy and Resources Committee with the leader of the majority
   party as Chairman
▽ an influential Performance Review Sub-Committee
▽ a powerful majority-party Policy Steering Group, which in practice acts as
   the majority party's cabinet
▽ four programme committees with logical broad areas of responsibility
▽ the clarification of the rôles of Council Chairman, leader, committee
   chairmen, and leader of the opposition
▽ a major induction and training programme, and appropriate support
   services, for elected members.

The political guidance on medium-term strategy is being secured in
Braintree District Council through the establishment of the Policy Action
Group as a sub-committee of the Policy Committee. It is multi-party and meets
both formally and informally.

A more fundamental way forward was recommended to Cambridgeshire
County Council by consultants Kinsley Lord in 1989. The consultants first
contemplated the complete abolition of service committees and their
replacement with client group committees; but that idea was thwarted by
legislative requirements. However, the recommendations retained the idea of
panels with a client focus, existing alongside service committees. The
suggested functions of the various councillor bodies were described as follows:

▽ **Council** (77 members)
   — sets constitutional framework
   — fixes rate and determines strategic issues
   — determines major service and controversial corporate issues, following
   recommendations of Policy or Service Committees
   — holds Policy Committee to account.

▽ **Policy Committee** (about 14 members)
   — provides strategic focus for the Council
   — formulates budget proposals and Medium-Term Plan for Council to
   determine
   — sets framework of policies and standards on a corporate basis
   — defines what client needs should be met and allocates funds/
   recommends allocation of funds accordingly (taking account of input from
   Select Panels)
   — individual members will have specific operational remit e.g. for
   Education, for Transportation, etc.
   — directs the operation of Select Panels.

▽ **Select Panels** (about 7–10 members each — but could be varied)
   — some standing, but mostly time-specific, diverse and task- orientated
   — limited in total number
   — primary role of challenging, questioning, and advocating, in the
   context of explicit policy direction
   — changing focus on particular client groups from time to time e.g. could
   target corporate policy themes
   — maintaining close contacts with client groups
   — monitoring performance of service providers on the ground in terms of
   how well they are meeting client needs

— harnessing local member experience and knowledge.

▽ **Service Committees** (14 members each)
— no sub-committees (with [a few] specific exceptions...)
— identify Medium-Term Plan and budget priorities and express views on policy options to Policy Committee
— determine service policy issues (policies will be explicit to facilitate effective operation of Select Panels)
— oversee controversial operational issues
— define performance, as an extension of policy, and monitor attainment.

The common theme of all these examples is that strategic change means organisational change, and that organisational change itself must embrace member as well as officer structures.

A framework for action

Beyond structures, a basic requirement is to ensure that the strategic plan sits within an overall set of processes that link strategy to action through plans and budgets. Unless strategic planning is both seen as, and used as, one part — albeit an important one — in an overall management process, the aspirations and guidelines that the strategic plan contains will materialise as no more than pious statements. Chapter one touched on the contribution of medium-term plans in this regard.

The importance of the links between different processes are explicitly acknowledged by a number of authorities. Wiltshire County Council, for instance, examined a range of planning and management processes within the context of its decision in 1988 to tackle the production of a 'Council Strategy'. The planning cycle adopted frames the strategic plan as one of the stages in a general thrust that is aimed at, and concerned with, better service delivery. The ten stages are:

		To be revised
▽	Statement of Committee Needs and Objectives	Annually
▽	Statement of Committee Performance Indicators	Possibly annually
▽	County Trends Document	Annually
▽	Key Issues for the County Council	When strategy is altered
▽	Adoption of Strategy for the County Council	Probably every 3 years
▽	Budgeting	Annually
▽	Capital Programme Preparation	Annually
▽	Preparation of Service Plans by departments	Annually
▽	Performance Reports	Annually
▽	Policy Reviews	Ongoing

Cambridgeshire County Council has a well developed medium-term planning system, which allocates resources to committees, programme areas, and projects. It is now looking at developing clearer and more specific links between the 'Ten Year Outlook', the corporate strategy, and the action-based medium-term plan. The explicit links proposed are shown in Figure 6.1.

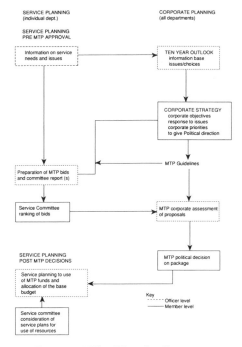

Figure 6.1 The Planning Processes
Source: Cambridgeshire County Council. 'Corporate Planning in Cambridgeshire:
A Position Statement — Autumn 1988'

From the outset, the move that Arun District Council made in introducing strategic planning was part of an integrated approach, which it has termed the 'corporate business system'. The Council's strategy statement or strategic plan has provided policy direction, but crucially has been linked directly to hard-edged decisions on service levels, organisation structure, and finance through a simple but comprehensive planning and management process.

Similarly, Wrekin District Council has developed clear management and planning arrangements that connect longer-term aspirations with shorter-term action, as well as linking implementation to direction.

However, hand in hand with 'operationalising' a strategy through turning it into something more detailed for a shorter timescale must go the translation of corporate intentions into plans for individual parts of the organisation. One way of looking at these plans is to divide them into service plans and business plans. Chapter five has already examined the relationship between corporate and service plans, pointing out that the latter sometimes exist without the former, but that each should pay regard to the other.

Business plans are different. The term is used here to denote plans for those parts of the organisation that can be viewed as in-house contractors, or business units. However strong the counter-argument might be, a case can be put forward for an individual sharp-end service to exist in its own right, aside from the rest of council services. But business units have no validity except as providers of services to the rest of the authority. They can be either support services (as in the case of business units concerned with activities such as cleaning, purchasing, design, building, printing, IT support, customer-led legal and financial support, and so on), or services available directly to an external customer but where another part of the organisation acts in a client role (as with highway maintenance, school meals, and in the future, sports and leisure centre management). For such units, plans must be wholly subordinate to the business needs of the authority.

Amongst the best examples of such business plans are those for the development of information systems and technology. Indeed, a survey by the Society of Information Technology Managers in 1988 revealed that 62% of British local authorities had produced a formal IT strategy. The cost of equipment and systems in cost-conscious local government, and the difficulty of recruiting and retaining computing professionals, put a premium on ensuring that scarce resources are put to best use, in accordance with corporate priorities. More fundamentally, authorities have come increasingly to be aware that information processing is not just a tactical consideration at the detailed level of service delivery and back-up — it is also a strategic consideration with powerful implications for the shape of an organisation and the relationships within it.

Supportive management arrangements

Setting the strategic plan in an overall framework will still prove ineffective unless the wider range of management procedures and controls are in tune with the strategy, and are designed to help its implementation. This framework will have many elements, but amongst the more important are those commented on below.

SCHEMES OF DELEGATION

The importance of pushing responsibility down the line as a response to issues facing local government was stressed in Chapter four. One authority that is moving down that path in a determined way is Berkshire County Council. It has given about 700 cost centre managers (in addition to schools and colleges) more authority over the resources they deploy, coupled with corresponding accountability for achieving agreed targets. Over 40 cost centre managers were in 1989 participating in a pilot scheme to test out the possibilities, and more were to follow.

Such a strategy will be successful only if it is accompanied by a clear definition of authority and responsibility. Underlying the change to devolved management, therefore, is a parallel change in the rules for the day-to-day running of the Council, with an explicit hierarchy of objectives, increased clarity about service standards, individual responsibilities for achieving pre-set results, and an emphasis on monitoring performance.

Not only is it important to define responsibilities at each level: it is also important for such definitions to distinguish between the strategic and the tactical. Too often, schemes of delegation of responsibilities to both committees and officers fail to do so; and such lack of clarity only serves to hinder achievement of even the most modest strategic progress.

FINANCIAL REGULATIONS

A strategy that seeks to delegate responsibility and accountability needs to be supported by financial regulations that allow the delegation of financial decisions.

Surrey County Council has developed a system of financial management — praised by the Audit Commission as a model of good practice — that does just this. By relaxing the rules controlling the detailed use of resources, managers have been made accountable, and the 'ownership' of budgets has shifted from the Treasurer to departments. Pushing responsibility for budget management on to line managers has given them greater freedom but also forced them to accept responsibility for using their budgets effectively and keeping within them.

Of course, moves in this direction not only allow the development of delegated resource management — they also encourage more imaginative use of resources, and provide an incentive to improved efficiency where resources freed up can be retained and redeployed.

PERSONNEL CONTROLS

Just as the strait-jacket of too many financial decisions being taken at the centre is being loosened in many authorities, so systems for approving the creation of extra posts or changes in conditions of service are also tending to be revised to reflect advances in strategic management. In Warwickshire County Council, for example, the only controls over staffing numbers now exercised directly by a central committee are in relation to major departmental restructurings, or significant departures from agreed policies.

PAY STRUCTURES

There is increasing movement throughout local government to relate pay to performance. Traditionally, this has been confined to manual workers through incentive bonus schemes — but no longer. The trend is now towards performance-related pay for white collar staff.

The approaches adopted vary, with differences existing over which categories of staff are included, whether the reward for good performance is through a lump sum bonus or basic salary increase, and whether national pay scales are abandoned or simply used in a flexible way. But whatever the differences in detail, the thrust is the same — a form of strategic management that emphasises the achievement of pre-defined targets, i.e. the effective implementation of plans.

Developing the management culture

Strategic planning highlights areas of change and new directions. The more fundamental the change and the more unfamiliar the directions, the more vital it is to ensure that the organisation has a culture that supports rather than obstructs. Since managers are at the hub of ensuring the implementation of change, their attitudes are crucial. If managers are not:

▽   convinced that change is on the way

▽ committed to bringing about desirable change
▽ committed to responding to unavoidable change
▽ equipped to confront change

the chances of success are slim indeed. That is why a local authority's
management development strategy and training policies need to be grounded
in its strategic planning objectives, and reflect:

▽ what sort of local authority it is aiming to be
▽ how it is striving to change.

Gloucestershire County Council has made significant progress in
translating policy planning and priority setting into operational objectives and
job definitions. Its overall strategy is linked directly to individual staff
development through a clear, integrated process.

▽ Three-year priority objectives: each committee publishes three-year
   objectives.
▽ Annual Key Tasks : every committee publishes a list of key tasks for the
   year ahead; progress in achieving them is reviewed in the course of the
   year.
▽ Departmental Work Programmes : all departments have work
   programmes which are used internally to monitor performance during the
   year.
▽ Staff Development Interviews : at least once a year, every member of staff
   has the opportunity to discuss with his/her manager how work is
   progressing; to consider future priorities; to assess the effectiveness of
   management support; and to explore future training and development
   needs.

Another good example can be found in the London Borough of Bromley,
whose Management Bulletin clearly shows how the Council's 'new
management style' links to the management development strategy (see Fig.
6.2).

Conclusion

By no means all the examples of encouraging practice mentioned in this
chapter arose from decisions about how best to implement a strategic plan.
Indeed, the distinction between what should be in a plan, what is needed to
implement it, and what is needed to stimulate its preparation can become very
blurred. What is important, however, is that a strategic plan does not exist in
isolation — that is a recipe for failure.

Review questions

▲ Do your authority's management and political structures encourage or
   hinder a strategic approach?
▲ Does it have a set of planning processes that turn strategy into more
   detailed plans?
▲ Does it have a clear statement of responsibilities — between committees
   and officers, for departments and sections, and for individual officers?

STEPS TO BETTER MANAGEMENT

1. **March 85** Policy & Resources Committee adopts report defining our management style. Chief Executive, Nigel Palk, begins lectures promoting the "new style".

Aug 85 New corporate image based on logo "Bromley — the London Borough." Corporate design group formed to develop new image.

Sustaining mid career interest!

3. **Sept 86** Policy & Resources Committee identifies four elements of "new style" for further promotion (see opposite).

Nov 86 Management training budget expanded: residential courses for senior managers; in house CMS for junior managers.

Jan 87 Corporate Design Manual launched – guidelines for presenting a better image to the public.

More money for training our managers

5. **Oct 88** Performance statements linked to performance related pay for some senior officers.

Jan 89 Customer Service Programme launched: backed by guidelines, staff newspaper and "service days".

June 89 Management style booklet updated to reflect new pressures — competition, accountability, greater consumer choice, etc.

2. **Sept 85** Introduction of "action learning" based training programmes for managers.

Nov 85 In house "Management Bulletin" launched.

Jan 86 Management style booklet published. Start of annual appraisal scheme for managers.

4. **May 87** Streamlined departmental structure approved.

Oct 87 Performance statements introduced — key accountabilities for managers defined.

May 88 Annual training plans brought in for all departments.

Looking to the Future

Figure 6.2 Steps to Better Management
Source: London Borough of Bromley

▲ Do schemes of delegation distinguish between the strategic and the tactical?

▲ Do its financial and personnel control systems stifle or encourage strategic change?

▲ Is management development linked to what the council wants to achieve?

7 Checking on progress

Key points

▲ Strategies must be reviewed to keep them up to date.
▲ That means keeping abreast of the factors that prompted the strategy in the first place.
▲ It also means keeping tabs on progress and performance in implementing the strategy.
▲ Performance measurement also has a somewhat separate rôle as a means of securing better value for money.

Keeping up with change

Unforeseen change

The central theme of this book is that the world of local government is changing so much that some sort of a strategy is needed if that change is to be confronted successfully. However, the point has already been made that we are concerned not only with changes that are already upon us or that can confidently be predicted. For, with the pace of change being so rapid, local government must expect to have to contend with fresh challenge after fresh challenge, including many whose nature cannot be forecast with any certainty at all until they are actually upon us.

One possible response is to engage in longer-term speculation, attempting to look further ahead than the period of only a few years that usually provides the basis for a strategy. With the recent dominance of Conservative party philosophy on the national scene, this search for a vision of a more distant future for local government has focused attention on the views of prominent organisations such as the Institute for Economic Affairs and the Adam Smith Institute. These organisations can boast an impressive record over the last decade of having their proposals adopted and predictions fulfilled. But if the changes affecting local government cannot all necessarily be foreseen well in advance, then nor can the political complexion of central government. So a more reliable course is to leave room for alternative visions — for building various scenarios, rather than putting all one's forecasting eggs in one basket.

This is the case for contingency planning. But the topic is easier to talk about than undertake; and, as was mentioned in Chapter four, examples of contingency planning in local authorities' strategic plans are hard to come by. Are there no other ways that the strategy itself can respond to unforeseen change? It can, of course, put emphasis on ways of making an authority:

▽ aware of the prospect of further unknown change

▽   psychologically prepared to face up to further change
▽   even welcome the challenge of change.

But the outcome of that can be no more than a change in attitude: it does not bring about action. It therefore follows that, as a strategy cannot easily get to grips with unforeseen change, it must at least be altered when necessary as the nature of further change becomes clearer and more definite. In other words, it must be kept up-to-date; and it is this topic — review — that provides the focus for this chapter.

Reviewing pressures for change

A strategy is built on estimates and forecasts, as well as speculation, assumption, and assertion (see Chapter four). This environment is not stable; it is dynamic. Changes that occur may well call into question the strategy itself. These changes, therefore, need to be measured and monitored to test whether that is the case.

In doing this, the danger of over-elaboration must be guarded against. Because strategy addresses key issues over the longer term, it is relatively robust. It is not particularly sensitive to small changes, for example, in the size and structure of population or to differences of tens or even hundreds of thousands of pounds in the amount of financial resources becoming available. But without some amendment it is very unlikely to cope with a change in political direction or a substantial shift in population trends.

Like the strategy, therefore, the monitoring process needs to be selective. That means:

▽   picking out the principal factors which condition the shape of the strategy, and concentrating on monitoring those
▽   checking their progress regularly but not too frequently
▽   instituting a review if there is a major change in any of the principal factors. That is particularly true of political or legislative changes that may well strike at the general strategic thrust
▽   in any case every three or four years asking fundamental questions about the continuing relevance of the strategy.

This strategic approach to monitoring should ensure that it does not become a burdensome paper-chase, which certainly in the days of corporate planning put continued commitment to planning itself in serious jeopardy.

Most authorities that conduct regular reviews seem to have learned this lesson, and ensure that they are short and to the point.

▽   Gloucestershire County Council updates its 'Gloucestershire Review' annually. It feeds into the annual budget strategy, influencing decisions on the allocation of resources between services.
▽   Cambridgeshire County Council revises its 'Ten Year Outlook' each year. This is used as a background to the annual review of the Corporate Strategy, which in turn influences decisions on which items to include in the Medium Term Plan at its annual roll-forward.

Some authorities set out to review change factors less frequently.

▽ Braintree District Council's 'The Way Forward: Policy Objectives and Plans' was not reviewed until two years after its production.
▽ Arun District Council produced a document entitled 'Strategy Papers and Programme Plan 1987–91'. This was intended to guide action over the entire four-year life of the Council.
▽ Thamesdown Borough Council produced its 'A New Vision for Thamesdown — Strategy Statement' in 1985, intending it to cover the whole of the mid-to-late 1980s.

Needless to say, a strategy intended to remain unreviewed for a number of years runs more of a risk of not remaining relevant in a council without a majority party.

Checking performance

If local authorities have not been as advanced as they might have been in devising strategies and plans, they have been even less well advanced in introducing systems to check on progress and performance — the concept of performance review. This is true so far even in many of those authorities which embrace strategic planning enthusiastically.

But performance review needs to become an integral part of the well-run authority's set of management processes. In the words of Bill Taylor, Assistant Chief Executive of Rochdale MDC, 'whilst systematic performance review may have been thought of in the past as being "nice to have", it now falls into the "must have" category'.

Not surprisingly, this theme is echoed strongly by the Audit Commission: 'an authority needs to check how well its existing set-up is working ... it also needs to determine if change is required and identify priority tasks to secure the better implementation of that change. Priority tasks can then be projected forward to provide the basis of a plan, the implementation of which is then monitored and reviewed' ('Performance Review in Local Government — Action Guide'). This is illustrated in Figure 7.1.

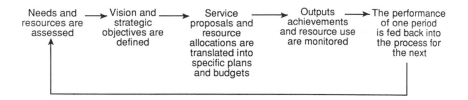

Figure 7.1 Checking Performance
Source: Audit Commission 'Performance in Local Government — Action'

Strategic planning moves a local authority from focusing on the routine of service delivery onto being concerned with and about direction and achievement. Performance review is the natural complement which reinforces and completes the process. Certainly, when it is in place, it gives not only managers but also councillors the handles of the real levers of management. It reveals whether and where progress is being made, and points to where concerted action is needed to unblock log-jams.

But the process of performance review is far-reaching. It must stretch into the nooks and crannies of all services. It is both demanding and a great consumer of information and statistics. The dangers are therefore all too obvious:

▽   the risk of the system collapsing under the weight of information
▽   the ease with which attention can be concentrated on qualities that are measurable, while ignoring equally important — or perhaps even more important — aspects that do not lend themselves to statistical analysis
▽   the potential for focusing on how much activity is going on (inputs) rather than the extent to which the problem is being solved (outcomes)
▽   the information collection process becoming an end in itself, so that although performance may be measured the measurement is unrelated to any prospect of action
▽   the system becoming mechanistic and the underlying challenging and questioning purpose correspondingly lost.

These dangers can be avoided if they are addressed. Within the context of strategic planning, however, the greatest danger is that comprehensive performance review will obscure the strategic. The attainment of key objectives will be masked in a plethora of data about the attainment of service objectives generally.

Wiltshire County Council has recognised this dilemma in the major exercise that it has embarked upon to introduce performance measurement across all the areas of Council service. It has produced a framework for performance review that distinguishes two levels:

▽   performance indicators measuring achievement of key objectives which will be set out in the Council's five-year Policy Plan
▽   performance indicators measuring achievement of targets set for individual services.

This hierarchical arrangement allows the generality of service objectives to nestle within an overall strategic framework, while the full momentum of performance review is maintained.

In some other authorities the approach to performance review has been less comprehensive, with the focus of attention concentrating on strategic achievements.

▽   Devon County Council carries out a review of its 'Devon Strategy to 1990' each summer. This process examines the extent to which individual strategies have been achieved and what remains to be done, and leads to the strategy being amended accordingly.
▽   Northamptonshire County Council considers a monitoring report each autumn on its Medium Term Plan. This focuses on:
      — the Medium Term Plan's key indicators
      — comparisons with other authorities, using the Audit Commission's profile of the Authority and CIPFA statistics.

However, councils where any sort of monitoring and review are central to the style and direction of management are rare. Certainly there are few authorities where performance measurement features as a crucial element of regular committee business.

One of the best examples of an exception is Bexley London Borough Council. Each year, targets are set for each department; and these are then monitored every quarter, with a monitoring report being submitted to the relevant service committee. At the end of the year, performance against the year's targets is reviewed to assess how far committee objectives have been met. This process is illustrated in Fig. 7.2, which also shows how monitoring is inextricably linked to other elements of the Council's 'Business Process'.

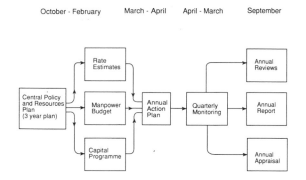

Figure 7.2 Bexley's Business Process
Source: Bexley London Borough Council 'The Business Process'

Another exception is Arun District Council, which also lays great emphasis on monitoring performance during the course of the year. Figure 7.3 shows the relationship of the Authority's monitoring and review activities to its overall 'Corporate Business System'.

However, it may not be long before these exceptions become the rule. For recent attention devoted to the search for useful performance indicators has led a number of other authorities to put increasing emphasis on them. One example is Berkshire County Council, which has begun to use indicators to monitor performance in a hierarchy of explicit business plans:

▽   departmental business plans
▽   120 service area business plans
▽   700 cost centre business plans.

This trend is growing as outside factors — particularly central government initiatives — begin to pressurise local government into taking a critical look at the quality of services.

▽   As schools and colleges gain increased responsibility for managing their own affairs under the Education Reform Act, education authorities will have to put added emphasis on monitoring both the educational and managerial performance of individual establishments. Figure 7.4 sets out the factors for which performance indicators are expected to be needed. Given the slow progress that has been made in the past in devising useful and acceptable performance indicators in the education service, very rapid

progress is being required in introducing this change of role. The speed of
that progress is bound to spill over into other local government services,
where the measurement of performance has made little — if any — more
headway.

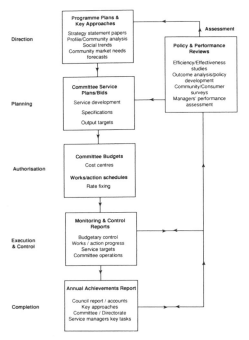

Figure 7.3 Arun's Corporate Business System
Source: Arun District Council 'Strategy Papers and Programme Plans 1987–1991'

▽   Contract monitoring is, of course, an inescapable linchpin of the way local
authorities have to operate in the competitive climate introduced by the
Local Government Act 1988. The skills already exercised by, for example,
highways, building design, and purchasing professionals are now needed
much more widely within client departments in their relations with
contractors. What is more, the emphasis on performance monitoring is
just as necessary if the contractor is an in-house direct service organisation
as if it is an outside contractor.

▽   In the same way, the move towards the greater accountability of support
functions to front-line functions means that the latter will increasingly
need to monitor the former's performance in a methodical way, perhaps
against formal service level agreements. Just as education authorities will
be monitoring schools' performance, so will schools be monitoring the
service they get from councils in fields such as grounds maintenance,
purchasing, information technology support, job advertising — and so on!

The conclusion is simple: the new roles for local authorities leave
them no choice but to pay more regard in the future to monitoring
performance. Even where this is carried out primarily for reasons of
accountability or control, the result will be to provide information and
skills that will be invaluable in reviewing strategies.

Input Considerations:

(a) **Pupil intake**   Social-economic background
                       Cultural background
                       Innate ability
                       Handicaps
                       Levels of expectation by
                         pupils and parents
                       Academic attainment on
                         entry to each phase

(b) **Resources**   Number of teachers, by grade
                       Number of support staff by
                         type

(c) **Background**   Parental support (financial
                         and otherwise)
                       Book and library provision
                       Technical facilities
                       Recurrent expenditure by type
                       Accommodation levels and
                         standards
                       Historical background
                       Stability of organisation

Process Indicators:

(a) **Staff**   Teachers' characteristics,
                         including qualifications
                       Staff demeanour
                       Staff sick leave
                       Teacher turnover

(b) **Teacher   Contact ratios
    deployment**   Class sizes
                       Mismatch (subject,
                         experience, training)

(c) **Curriculum   Core subject provision
    arrangements**   Non-core subject options
                       Particularised provision
                       Examination options
                       Curriculum co-ordination
                       Curriculum documentation

(d) **Wider   Provision of pastoral system
    educational   Structured sporting activities
    practices**   Activities for the local
                         community
                       Links with industry and commerce
                       Extra-curricula cultural
                         activities

(e) **Organisation**   Management delegation commitment
                       Pupil grouping provision
                       Homework policy and its
                         applications
                       Involvement of governors

(f) **Mutuality**   Level of expectation of teachers
                       Level of responsibility given to
                         pupils
                       Rewards/sanctions punishment
                         systems

Outcome Indicators:

(a) **Intermediate**   Pupils' demeanour
                       Attendances, absenteeism, truancy
                       Lateness
                       Performance in internal activities
                       Participation in external activities
                       Indictable offences recorded

                       Participation in sporting, social,
                         cultural activities post 16
                       Uptake of initial employment
                         (relative to location)
                       Employment status at ages 21 and 25
                       The views of potential employers

(b) **Final for   Performance in external
    secondary   examinations by age 16
    schools**   Other intellectual attainments
                       Entry rates into continued and
                         further education at age 16
                       Performance in external examinations
                         from post-compulsory education

(c) **Final for   Academic attainments at age 11
    primary   Participation in sporting, social,
    schools**   cultural activities post 11

Figure 7.4 Performance Indicators in Schools
Source: Cooper and Lybrand 'Local Management of Schools', Crown copyright

Searching for improvements

Some authorities have tackled performance measurement in a way designed to focus primarily on value-for-money improvements in services. The emphasis should be on selective analysis and examination of issues; and in the best examples this leads to, or is linked to, a broader policy framework which contains some, if not all, the elements of effective strategic planning.

In this particular field, Suffolk County Council has been a leader with its Service Priority Review process. Interestingly, the origins of this process can be traced back to a budgeting procedure (Priority Base Budgeting, which itself grew out of Zero Base Budgeting), a fact which provides further evidence of just how closely linked are the various elements of an overall management system. Within Suffolk, the system has close relations with the strategic planning process (which now has its expression in a Medium Term Plan), as is shown in Figure 7.5.

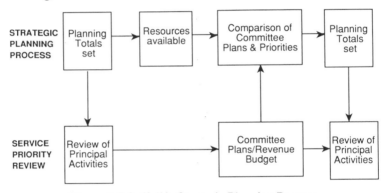

Figure 7.5 Suffolk's Strategic Planning Process
Source: Suffolk County Council 'Service Priority Review — A manual for members and officers'

Suffolk's Service Priority Review is a comprehensive process with the following objectives:

▽ to achieve a high degree of understanding of needs, policies and services
▽ to ensure that resources are deployed economically, efficiently, and effectively
▽ to review and, if appropriate, change established priorities for expenditure
▽ to provide a framework within which medium-term planning can take place.

It involves:

▽ the definition of activities and their objectives by service department managers
▽ the identification of:
    — trends in needs, expected resources, etc,
    — possible alternative levels of service quality and volume (eg the minimum acceptable, the current level, and at least one higher level)
    — possible alternative methods of service delivery
▽ selection by councillors of activities for closer examination
▽ ranking by councillors of the alternatives in order of priority

▽ consideration by councillors of whether the resources available to the service are being put to the best use
▽ consideration by councillors of what additional resources should be spent on if they become available to the service.

An allied approach has been adopted by Avon County Council, which embarked on a range of closely linked policy and performance review activities in 1986. These included the production by all departments of 'position statements' under the following headings:

▽ operational objectives
▽ current policy/programmes
▽ standard of provision needed to achieve objective
▽ current resources/shortfall
▽ performance indicators.

The approach has proved a more effective way of identifying areas for review than the previous emphasis on comparisons with other authorities.

Northumberland County Council also adopted a new review process of a broadly similar kind in the late 1980s, in this case called Service Assessment and Review. As with many of the review processes described here, Service Assessment and Review is intended to fit into a wider decision-making context, and to:

▽ provide an authority-wide framework for medium term planning
▽ lead to the identification of corporate priorities and issues.

The stages of the process are as follows:

Stage	*Purpose*
1. Departments to define their principal activities and sub-activities.	To provide a clear and comprehensive statement of each Department's work and to identify areas of overlap or duplication.
2. Departments to provide a clear set of objectives for each activity for the subsequent financial year and for an extended (five year) planning period. An indication of the priority attached to each activity and anticipated changes in priority should also be provided.	To set a policy framework for departmental activities and priorities.
3. Departments to select:	
a. activities where increased service provision is essential (rather than desirable) over the extended planning period;	To provide a means for the critical examination of current activity patterns in line with objective and priority statements set out above.

b. activities which could diminish as a
   result of reduced 'client' demand
   or changed priorities; and

c. activities where 'no change' is
   appropriate.

4.	Departments to identify the 'key' issues from their service both currently and for the extended planning period.	To concentrate attention and subsequently effort on selected areas or activities where overview is necessary to accommodate changed circumstances or anticipated changes.
5.	Departments to determine 'key' areas for achievement for the subsequent financial year and extended planning period and to establish operational targets by which achievement can be monitored.	To establish departmental priorities and workable targets by which members, officers, and clients can monitor progress systematically.

It is interesting to note that Avon and Northumberland County Councils (and Leicestershire County Council, which uses a technique similar to Suffolk's) used the review process as the starting point for breaking into the planning and review cycle.

Structures for review

Chapter five discussed to what extent strategic planning at officer level should be a centralised function. Similar considerations apply with review processes, where practice in different authorities varies widely from wholly centralised to wholly decentralised arrangements. The most common arrangement seems to be a combination of central and departmental involvement, reflecting the twin advantages of:

▽ having someone at the centre to
   — to maintain an overview, and
   — make it harder for departments to sweep unsavoury matters under the carpet
▽ tapping into the depth of knowledge that only the department under review can possess.

Just as enlightening are arrangements at councillor level. A performance review sub-committee was something that most self-respecting authorities felt unable to do without following the Bains Report of 1972. But numerous authorities have found performance review a remarkably hard political process, not least when it entails a central committee 'interfering' openly and in detail with the work of service committees.

A variety of responses can therefore be encountered. Some authorities still put the emphasis on a central performance review committee: Gloucestershire County Council, for example, re-established one in the late 1980s. Some, such as the London Borough of Kingston-on-Thames, have decided that review is purely a management task, in which members should not be involved. Others have decentralised responsibility for review to service committees. An interesting example is Avon County Council, where each service committee has a policy and service review sub-committee to review policies and performance (see Fig. 7.6).

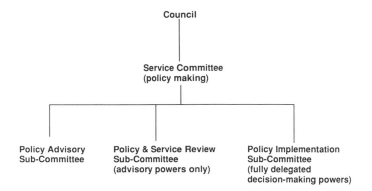

Figure 7.6 Structures for Review
Source: D. Latham 'Climate for Change: County Councils Gazette Aug. 1988'

The process is not wholly decentralised, however, as the central Resource Co-ordination Committee also has a policy & service review sub-committee, responsible for encouraging and monitoring other committees' review activities, and dealing with issues that cross service committee boundaries.

Maintaining the momentum

The history of corporate planning has taught us to guard against complacency, and against procedure overtaking purpose. Where the process of strategic planning and review has already taken, or is taking, root the lessons should not be forgotten.

At its most basic, the clear message is that effective and successful review is not just about:

▽ performance indicators
▽ officer and member groups

but at least as much about making sure that

▽ the organisation — both departmental and committee — is still the one best suited to delivering the council's targets
▽ people have the qualities that implementation of the strategy demands: that 'doers' can become 'enablers', for example, and that the necessary support and training is put in place to help them do so
▽ the financial, personnel, and other systems and processess are geared towards achieving the changes the council wants and not to frustrating them.

To achieve this means ensuring that periodically there is a thorough-going review where these questions, which strike at the very heart of strategy, are asked.

There are indications up and down the country that the climate within local government is changing in a way that reinforces challenge to the status quo. However, the gravest indictment of local government's managerial competence is that it has largely taken outside intervention — especially legislation or threatened legislation — to raise the profile of strategic and performance review, and to have the issue taken seriously at all widely.

Review questions

▲ Is your authority regularly producing information about how the factors that help change its services are themselves changing?
▲ Does it have systems to set targets and review progress?
▲ Does it develop attitudes amongst managers that question performance?
▲ Does the organisation of your Council and Committee business help members discuss service quality?
▲ What officer and member bodies have responsibility for evaluating performance of services?
▲ Does your council undertake a thorough-going review of its strategy every few years?

8 How do councillors benefit?

Key points

▲ Strategic planning is an essential ingredient in helping councillors to take charge of the direction in which the local authority is moving, by providing the opportunity to inject the political agenda for change into the management process.

▲ But, to make the most of the opportunity, councillors need to consider how they are organised and what roles they are seeking to play.

▲ It is not all plain sailing, though. Although no less relevant in 'hung' councils, it can prove harder there.

▲ And explicitness about future intentions does bring the danger of exposing failure and alerting political opposition.

Much of what is said in earlier chapters is from the perspective of the council as a whole. This chapter and the next two attempt to narrow the focus, and to pull together some threads relating to particular groups.

Helping councillors manage the future

Chapter one sketched the background for local government in which substantial change is inevitable as a result of:

▽ legislation
▽ market forces
▽ population and social trends
▽ awakening consumerism
▽ tight finance.

The choice for councillors is not whether their councils should change, but whether they wish:

▽ to anticipate those changes
▽ and, by doing so, to be in the driving seat and address those changes in a pro-active way that maximises the chances of the council influencing events rather than just reacting to them.

The gamut of pressures on councillors conspire against this forward-thinking.

▽ The mass of routine business crowds out discussion of vision and policy.

Almost all committee agendas in virtually any local authority bear testimony to this.

▽ Budget discussions are part of an annual hurly-burly of rate-fixing, in which short-term considerations usually dominate.

▽ Simply coping with, and reacting to, the welter of government legislation and regulations, as well as all the other pressures for change, is as much as many councillors can get to grips with.

▽ The rapid turnover of councillors makes it difficult for them to get on top of the mass of ad hoc information. In one council, the percentage of councillors standing down voluntarily increased from 15% in 1977 to nearly 70% in 1989.

▽ Particularly in 'hung' councils, much of the political effort is consumed in simply making sure that the administration keeps going.

▽ Short-term thinking is reinforced by the election process, particularly in those authorities where that is an annual event.

Clearly, it is not easy to combat these pressures, to get on top, and to succeed in articulating a direction which:

▽ gives clear guidance on what is to be achieved
▽ is based on sound operational principles
▽ is accepted as authoritative by council committees and other bodies
▽ controls effectively how the strategy is to be implemented.

Strategic planning can offer a lifeline. By its very nature:

▽ it provides a flow of information to councillors that hits the strategic rather than the normal routine level
▽ it focuses on key issues and targets and so helps councillors do the same
▽ it gives councillors the opportunity to make sure the agenda is the same as their own
▽ it forces discussion of the role of councillors and political organisation both onto the agenda and towards the top of it.

The information flow is important. Too often committee agendas are driven by events rather than policy, and force councillors to examine council services through the wrong end of a telescope. The work involved in preparing a strategic plan helps them to get away from that, and to look across the board at strategic issues.

For example, in Warwickshire County Council the work involved in preparing a strategic plan for the first time has put on the agenda for discussion — both formally and informally — by councillors:

▽ the type of role it wants to play in the future — ranging from direct service provider to contractor and entrepreneur
▽ new roles for elected members and officers, designed to sustain the health of local democracy but deliver high quality services and give good value for money
▽ the hard choices about priorities against the prospects of increasingly tight finances.

In Northamptonshire County Council, member discussion after the 1985 election identified seven principles to drive their medium-term planning process. Councillor and political thinking is now directed towards these issues, and their impact on the Council and its services. The normal procedure for putting together committee agendas would never have achieved the same attention for policy and future direction.

New ways of working

For councillors to be able to seize fully the opportunities strategic planning offers them to guide the process of change, they need to take a hard look at:

▽   how best to organise themselves to examine and determine policy
▽   their own role as elected members.

There is widespread evidence that where local authorities are involved in strategic planning, this is indeed happening.

The conventional committee structure is hardly conducive to innovative and imaginative thinking about policy issues. Councillors need time and information to contemplate and discuss. The success of most committees is measured in terms of the numbers of decisions made.

However, the London Borough of Bexley has developed a two-tier committee structure. The main committees have a strategic role in that they deal with broader policy matters and resource allocation for groups of services. By contrast, the sub-committees are mostly concerned with operational matters. Moreover, it is possible to be a member of a sub-committee without being on the main committee. In this way the different interests of members are catered for. Figure 7.6 showed a comparable arrangement in Avon County Council.

Chapter six describes a proposal currently being considered by Cambridgeshire County Council for member panels with a client-group focus to complement service committees. The Council had already developed a system for complementing formal committees with less formal member and officer groups for policy discussion. This practice is becoming more widespread, and is particularly well developed in Newcastle City Council, where at the last count there were no less than 60 informal officer and member sub-groups or working parties.

This move towards informal officer and member joint consideration of policy issues is also reflected in the increasing occurrence of 'away-days'. These are days set aside for informal officer/member discussion, often away from council premises.

A loosening up is also occurring in political structures. For example, Berkshire County Council has formally constituted party groups which are attended either by the Assistant Chief Executive or Assistant County Secretary together with service chief officers as necessary.

Chapter six mentioned that in some local authorities the role of members themselves is being reviewed. In 'The Competitive Council', the Audit Commission suggested four main strands to the councillor's role:

▽   policy formulation
▽   operational management
▽   performance review
▽   representation.

But Wiltshire County Council has gone much further and suggested a twelve-point job description for councillors.

1. To represent the people of Wiltshire and Wiltshire interests within the statutory framework of the Council.
2. Specifically, to represent his/her own electors, including those who voted against him/her and those who did not vote at all, and to deal with problems, issues, and complaints raised by individual constituents.
3. To represent the aims of his/her political party if he/she belongs to one.
4. To participate in the work of the committees and external organisations to which the Council appoints him/her.
5. To ensure the administration of the Council is both fair and efficient, and to contribute towards developing new ways of securing economy, effectiveness, and efficiency in delivering council services.
6. To be mindful of the Council's image, remembering always that members are the public face of the Authority.
7. To identify and approve measures designed to establish the needs of consumers of the Council's services.
8. To promote the recruitment and retention of good staff at all levels and the development of personnel policies to maintain and improve staff morale, recognising the importance of the member-officer relationship.
9. To keep under review the committee and staffing structures of the Council; to ensure they remain appropriate to the Council's needs; and to attempt to develop flexible structures capable of being easily adapted to changing needs.
10. In pursuit of good management, to ensure that decisions are taken at the lowest level commensurate with their importance.
11. To ensure that complaints against the Council are taken seriously and investigated properly.
12. To keep and sustain what is useful in the traditions of the authority and to reject any practices or services retained purely out of sentiment.

All of this activity is directed at putting elected members at the heart of discussion about and formulation of policy. Strategic planning offers the opportunity, but new ways of elected members acting and organising are needed to extract full advantage from it.

Helping councillors as politicians

Local government has become increasingly organised on party political lines. The research undertaken for the Widdicombe Committee showed this to be the case in more than 80% of all councils.

By definition, therefore, the vast majority of councillors are elected with a personal commitment to the manifesto of the political party to which they belong. Invariably the manifesto will promise the local electorate changes in the quality and quantity of services provided by the local authority, as well as changes in direction or organisation of the authority itself. However, unless those aspirations become linked firmly into the management and planning process of the local authority, the chances of attainment are slim indeed. It is perhaps worth recording that many chief officers have professed themselves convinced that councillors often fail to achieve their own political objectives because of the absence of any form of strategic planning process. Authority-wide strategic planning procedures are the medium through which political aspirations can be translated into practical targets.

What about strategic planning in a 'hung' council?

If strategic planning is one of the keys to achieving political success, there might be thought to be a question mark over its relevance to councils where no single party has an overall majority of seats. However, the changes that are occurring in local government still need driving, even if that drive does not flow out of the political manifesto of any one party. Strategic planning provides the framework which will still help members in 'hung' councils:

▽   get a handle on the pace and direction of change
▽   confront the fundamental change in local authority culture that legislation, and the new social and economic climate, are bringing
▽   take a longer-term look at where the authority is going.

If, as is suggested here, strategic planning is indeed relevant in the absence of overall political control, is it nonetheless feasible? There can be no denying the fact that many in local government are convinced that the answer is 'no', and that many speak from experience. Indeed, the view has entered the realm of conventional wisdom. No doubt there are 'hung' authorities where political factors are such as to thwart the introduction of strategic planning (although it is not only 'hung' authorities that can suffer from this condition!). And perhaps one should expect some lack of precision in the finished product. The strategy may be closer to a compass than a plan. However, this need not always be the case. For example, the planning process of Cambridgeshire County Council survived the disappearance of overall control in 1985, and changes in direction were taken on board through the annual roll-forward.

Those still unconvinced should look to the overall picture for encouragement. It is during the late 1980s that the loss of overall control has become so common, affecting a substantial minority of all councils and a majority of county councils; and that is exactly the period that has seen the re-emergence of strategic planning. Indeed, some authorities have contemplated and developed strategic planning for the first time only since becoming 'hung'.

The point is underlined by the fact that one third of all authorities referred to in this book are 'hung'.

An examination paper to fail?

The clarity that strategic planning brings to ideas for change also brings risks with it. Those risks entail giving advance notice of future intentions:

▽   **to political opposition**
    In one authority there is little doubt that the early publication of proposals of the proposed move to a wholly comprehensive education system forewarned the opposition party sufficiently for them to mount a formidable defence of the previous selective systems.

▽ **to lobbies and vested interests**
    In another authority the announcement of longer-term plans for action on
    the outcome of a fire risk-grading exercise prompted a vociferous
    campaign in defence of retained fire stations under threat of closure. For
    the most part that campaign proved successful.
▽ **to trade unions**
    In one city council the policy of moving from residential to community
    care for elderly people was frustrated in part by the action of trade unions
    representing staff affected by the closure of residential homes. There is
    little doubt that early knowledge of the proposals facilitated action against
    them.

Just as significantly, strategic plans make future proposals public in a way
that enables their success or achievement to be measured. The following
comment was made to us about one authority: '...(the proposal to embark on
strategic planning) was overtaken by a concern about being explicit...', and the
same message came from others. In an atmosphere of public political point-
scoring, setting targets — knowing that in practice some will not be attained —
is uncomfortable to say the least.

It would be arrogant for officers to tell councillors that the political price
was one that was worth paying; but officers could be forgiven for drumming
home the message that strategic planning helps councillors to be:

▽ informed
▽ in charge
▽ in front of change — so that problems are tackled before they become
    politically dangerous
▽ ready to change — giving some scope and flexibility to what they do.

Review questions

▲ Does your authority have a process that helps councillors to articulate
    their vision and goals?
▲ How are councillors given the opportunity to rise above the daily grind
    and to address longer-term issues?
▲ What arrangements are there to stimulate dialogue between officers and
    councillors on direction, priorities, and style?
▲ How many councillors could spell out what the council is trying to achieve
    over the next 3–4 years?
▲ Do your council's plans reflect political manifestos?

9 How do officers benefit?

Key points

▲ Some officers are hostile to strategic planning, claiming that it is unnecessary, impracticable, or undesirable.
▲ But there is a growing trend away from such views.
▲ This trend owes much to the realisation that strategic planning can enrich jobs by focusing attention on doing the right task and on broadening officers' horizons.
▲ It can also help bring about fairer rewards and a greater sense of belonging.
▲ But strategic planning must be kept useful through an emphasis on relevance and appropriate brevity.

Introduction

Much of this book has concentrated on the 'how' of strategic planning; and those parts that have looked at the 'why' have, on the whole, done so from the point of view of:

▽ local government as a whole
▽ a local authority as a whole

or, as with the last chapter:

▽ elected councillors.

But what of officers? It is they who almost invariably:

▽ assist councillors in defining the framework for a strategy
▽ gather background information
▽ draft a strategy for councillors to consider
▽ put together plans designed to translate strategy into action
▽ carry out those plans
▽ bring forward information to enable a strategy to be reviewed.

With such a degree of involvement, officers clearly need to be committed to what they are doing if strategic planning is to be more than an academic exercise of little effect. Perhaps it is not too cynical to suggest that the degree of commitment will depend in part on what is in it for them!

The case against

Chapters two and three have underlined the legacy of hostile attitudes that strategic planning is burdened with in local government. That hostility is certainly still to be found amongst many officers, and stems from the view that strategic planning is unnecessary, impracticable, and even undesirable.

Unnecessary?

Local authorities have been described as loose coalitions of semi-autonomous functions — a description depicted in Figure 4.1; and it is not hard to see why for many councils such a description has had — and still has? — more than a grain of truth in it. At the most basic level, the statutory authority for local government's activities stems from a very wide range of different Acts of Parliament, many of them dealing separately with different local government services. This reflects the way government departments are organised, with many of them having a direct interest in individual local government functions. This degree of interest is on occasion such as to call into question whether some local services are seen as more accountable to the Home Office, the Department of Transport, the Department of Education and Science, the Department of Trade and Industry, or the Department of Health than to the locally-elected council. Only the Department of the Environment and the Treasury attempt to complement these relations with an overall view of local government.

The structure of local authorities has tended to reinforce this state of affairs. Councillors have been divided into committees along service lines, with scarcely any thought to co-ordination before the all but universal advent of policy and resources committees in the early to mid 1970s. Departmental structures have tended to mirror committee structures, frequently with a one-to-one relationship; and officer career paths have underpinned the whole structure, with the emphasis firmly on narrow professionalism.

Over the last few years, there has been a trend amongst the local government professions to acknowledge the need for continuing professional development for their members. For there has been an increasing awareness that one of the weaknesses of professionalism is that people tend to continue to apply the knowledge they learned when qualifying, however much things might have changed since. But even when knowledge about facts and techniques is updated, the same is not always true of knowledge about ideas and pressures from outside the profession. The result can be a degree of ossification, and a slowness to respond to pressures for change.

Local government owes a great deal of what it has achieved to the high standards associated with professionalism. But professionalism has also brought with it a compartmentalised outlook, and a tendency to dwell on delivering more of the same, rather than to focus on inter-relationships and on changes around the corner. These legacies constitute an almost total negation of strategic planning as defined in Chapter one. It is therefore hardly surprising that for many local government professionals the idea of strategic planning does not score high marks for relevance.

When circumstances allow the relatively undisturbed continuation of the status quo, the necessity for strategic planning is not easy to demonstrate. And when resources are plentiful, and officers can see the expansion of empires without strategic planning, it is hard to demonstrate that developments could have been even more effective if backed by strategic planning. But when resources are scarce, and when fundamental changes are calling into question the quantity, nature, and even survival of much service delivery, attitudes tend to change; and it is no coincidence that the charge that strategic planning is unnecessary seems to be heard less frequently as officers contemplate the challenges of the late 1980s and early 1990s.

Impracticable?

The charge of impracticability is harder to refute. There *are* councils where the attitudes of members do not augur well for the success of strategic planning, for instance where:

▽ councillors' personal power-bases are firmly in service committees, militating against the pursuit of corporate goals
▽ councillors are preoccupied with parochial issues to the exclusion of wider matters
▽ councillors are reluctant to think beyond an imminent election.

Equally, there *are* difficulties that arise from uncertainties, both financial and political. It is undoubtedly harder to devise a plan when the resources available to implement it cannot be forecast with anything less than huge margins of error; and securing cross-party agreement on the content of a plan in a 'hung' council is a difficulty that cannot be lightly dismissed. Perhaps hardest of all to overcome is the officer view that the day-to-day pressures of service delivery simply do not allow time for involvement in strategic planning, however strong the arguments in favour of it.

Yet times are changing in local government. As the examples in this book show:

▽ officers in more and more authorities are attempting some form of strategic planning, despite the practical difficulties
▽ there is growing acceptance that financial uncertainty only serves to underline the importance of having a clear idea in advance of how to spend resources that become available at short notice
▽ a number of authorities have embarked on strategic planning despite having no overall political control
▽ the lesson is increasingly being learned that, unless one lifts one's sights above day-to-day preoccupations, one can easily fall prey to investing inordinate effort in the wrong thing altogether.

Undesirable?

To those officers who consider strategic planning unnecessary or impracticable must be added those who view it as actually undesirable. These include the departmental 'barons' of old, who see independence and opportunism as the hallmarks of their success, and who see that these would be threatened by any attempt to plan the affairs of the authority as a whole. But strategic planning does not assume a cosy corporate consensus. The desire to argue the case for one's own service at a time of ever scarcer resources is not only understandable but also legitimate. And the fact that so many services are facing common challenges and pressures underlines the sense of having a common strategic view within which relative priorities can be thrashed out.

Enriching the job

The right task

The creation of the Audit Commission in the early 1980s focused attention on the three famous 'E's: economy, efficiency, and effectiveness. The Commission's early publications tended to emphasise the first two, since they were easier to measure than the last. But, as the Commission itself came to acknowledge, such a limited focus can have a stultifying effect; and many local government officers — and councillors — have longed for more attention to be devoted to effectiveness: doing the right task rather than just doing the task right. This is one area where strategic planning can actually help enrich council officers' jobs, since it is all about deciding what the right task is and how to ensure that it can be carried out.

The results of failing to plan and co-ordinate work can have a profoundly harmful effect on staff morale. These results are all too common — yet are largely avoidable.

CHANGING DIRECTION NEEDLESSLY

Unless circumstances are unusually stable or strategies surprisingly far-sighted, changes of direction must be expected. The priority for next year may have ceased to be a priority by next decade. The problem may have gone away or been solved; the political philosophy may have altered. After a time, a strategy may actually come full circle. Such changes may bring a degree of frustration; but such frustration merely betrays a failure to understand that the world local government serves is a changing one, and that local government is about democracy and politics rather than about stability and continuity.

Changes of direction can also arise from the practice of trying things out and experimenting, and finding out that they do not work after all. It is one of the strengths of local government that ideas can be tested on a small scale in just one authority, in the knowledge that failure will not have a harmful impact across the country as a whole. On the other hand, successes can be adapted for use elsewhere. This is a very powerful method by which local government can make progress in all sorts of fields — a method substantially denied to central government.

However, unavoidable or beneficial changes of direction are one thing; it is quite another to be forced to change direction because the authority had merely drifted into a particular course of action without having thought out in advance how the action fitted into the overall scheme of things, or whether it was likely to be relevant to future circumstances. Little is more infuriating than to realise that one's efforts have been wasted because those in charge did not think through what was wanted.

PULLING IN OPPOSITE DIRECTIONS

In the absence of some sort of authority-wide strategy, there is no overall framework to guide people's activities, and to help ensure that they are all working towards a common end — or, at least, a collection of separate ends that are not actually in conflict with each other. The result can be a tremendously frustrating waste of effort as people actively — although perhaps unwittingly — counteract the effects of each other's work, even within a single organisation. Housing policies can undermine social services' policies on care for elderly people; planning policies can negate attempts to encourage economic development; nursery schooling decisions can work against child care programmes.

REINVENTING THE WHEEL

In the absence of the co-ordination that goes with an overall strategy, people beaver away in relative isolation. With luck, they may actually be heading in the same direction as each other — but they may be wholly unaware of it, and may therefore waste effort in duplicating each other's work. The scope for falling into this trap is wider than ever, as local government finds itself obliged to develop a series of new practices, such as drawing up detailed tender specifications under compulsory competition, and devising more direct internal charging mechanisms for internal support services. One way of minimising the risk, adopted by a number of authorities, is to bring together under common management the areas of work that face similar practices, for instance all direct service organisations. The cost of reinventing the wheel, and the benefits of co-ordination, are aptly illustrated in Figures 9.1 and 9.2.

Figure 9.1 Reinventing the Wheel
Source: Bill Plane, David Addyman, Chris Tabor — Warwickshire County Council

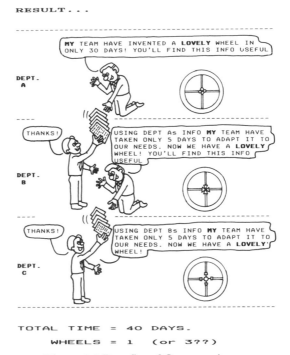

Figure 9.2 Benefits of Co-operation
Source: Bill Plane, David Addyman, Chris Tabor — Warwickshire County Council

STRAYING OFF THE CRITICAL PATH

A sound operational plan with its roots in strategy will identify the order in which things should be done, intermediate steps, and tools needed for the job. This is really no more than project planning writ large. Yet a failure to look ahead or pull strands together across departmental boundaries can mean that the necessary premises are not available in time for the new project staff, or trained staff are not available to operate the new computer system. Those who have worked hard in one area see their efforts thwarted. Present-day local government is on its mettle to see that these traps are avoided in facing the tight timetables associated with implementing the Education Reform Act, compulsory competition, and the community charge.

FAILING TO GET VITAL SUPPORT

Staying on the critical path requires not only that different parts of the organisation are meshed into each other in terms of timing, it also requires that they are addressing the same priorities. No amount of task programming will help if, for example, there is no strategy to ensure that the training function has an understanding of the skills needed to face future challenges. Some years ago, one authority discovered that its waiting list of 36 computer developments did not contain a single one related to its 10 top-priority strategic policies!

From the point of view of the local government officer, strategic planning can therefore be a powerful aid to ensuring that the right task is being carried out, and that common causes of frustration are avoided.

Broader horizons

Strategic planning also brings other positive benefits to employees, many of which are to do with broadening horizons and providing opportunities for contributing to the wider aims of the organisation. This is not a route favoured by all: some staff prefer to stay within the confines of their own profession or area of work, doing what they enjoy doing, have been trained to do, and are good at. The way local government is organised still allows room for many people with such an approach.

But the pace and fundamental nature of change within local government is increasingly putting a premium on staff who:

▽   can cope with change
▽   can switch to new areas of work and new ways of doing things
▽   know what is going on beyond their own neck of the woods (and can learn from it)
▽   understand where the organisation as a whole is heading.

This is, of course, particularly true of managers and aspiring managers. Fortunately, the signs are that employees increasingly see this need as stimulating rather than threatening.

One way in which this trend is being encouraged is through inter-service working. It is not that this is something new; but whereas joint working in the past often stemmed from a recognition by, say, two departments that there would be a mutual benefit in joint working on a particular topic, a strategic approach can actually identify such areas at an authority-wide level, rather than leaving it to departments to get their act together — or not, as the case may be. This does not necessarily mean the centre telling the sharp end what to do; what it does mean is a corporate decision to work together to achieve a corporate strategy.

Perhaps one of the most interesting examples that we have come across is how Cambridgeshire County Council has embarked upon a crime reduction strategy. The approach involves:

▽   targeting crimes and high risk areas
▽   injecting crime prevention as a high profile element in County Council work
▽   working closing with district councils
▽   involving local communities and voluntary groups
▽   reinforcing collaborative effort through a county co-ordinator working through inter-departmental, inter-authority, and inter-agency meetings.

The example is significant because it shows how the strategic approach to problem solving can highlight issues that the all-too-frequent 'tunnel-vision' simply lets fall between the cracks of separate policies and separate agencies.

A strategy, therefore, helps an organisation identify those topics that need a collaborative approach. However, a 'top-down' process of that sort need not stifle initiative. On the contrary, experience shows that encouraging people to operate beyond the narrower confines of their main area of work is a highly potent way of generating new ideas, encouraging innovation, and tapping unrealised potential. One such example is provided by Warwickshire County Council's customer awareness initiative. A broad strategy was set at top level by the chief officers' management team, but it was always recognised that successful implementation would depend (as with most initiatives) on actions at a lower level. A series of inter-departmental seminars was therefore arranged on the topic, and one of the conclusions reached by participants was the similarity of both diagnosis and prescription in different departments. As a result, teams were set up to take the initiative forward not only in each department, but also inter-departmentally; and many of the resulting actions apply across the authority.

The opportunities that strategic planning can offer for officers to broaden their horizons do not lie only in inter-departmental working. At a more basic — but no less important — level, the very process of producing a strategy can be very helpful in this direction. The point is well illustrated by Hampshire County Council. The 'Key Areas for Achievement' document sets out the main targets for development and change in the coming two years, with a section for corporate achievement and a section for each department. Third and fourth-tier officers provided the focus for preparing the document, and the draft was seen by about 300 staff. The process of preparing the document thus helped enormously with management communication, enabling departments to be aware of each other's agendas for change.

Fairer rewards

Chapter six discussed performance-related pay as one of the management arrangements that can help translate strategy into action. Relating pay to performance is not a universally popular concept; but the argument does seem to be gaining ground amongst officers, both for reasons of fairness, and also through the realisation that, in the challenging times that local government has entered, authorities can ill afford to carry passengers on their staff. This view is understandably most pronounced in direct labour organisations and direct service organisations, forced to compete for work against the private sector.

However, fairness has been — and still is, in some quarters — a sticking point as far as performance-related pay is concerned. There is understandable concern that the criteria for judging performance should minimise the scope for subjectivity, favouritism, personal animosity, and similar factors, to cloud judgment. It is here that a strategic approach to an organisation's activities can help. For an authority with little sense of direction has no objective way of assessing performance; whereas an authority with a strategy, and plans for its implementation, is likely to be in a position to set out targets not just for departments but also for individuals. Even where, for whatever reason, performance related pay has not been introduced, such targets can provide the basis for personal appraisal systems, so that members of staff know how they are doing. The greater clarity of purpose, and better feel for personal performance, provide a much sounder base from which individuals can plan their personal development and their future careers.

Sense of belonging

Many people joined local government because they wanted to provide a service to the community. They will have identified with the profession or department of which they were a part, and more broadly with a concept of public service delivered through a particular local authority. As the esteem in which local government as an institution is held by the general public has plummeted in recent years, it has become harder for employees to identify with public service as a concept or even with a particular local authority. Preparing people to meet the challenges described in Chapter one necessitates providing them with motivation; and, if that is not to be merely a narrow professional motivation of the sort touched on earlier in this chapter, that means re-establishing the organisation as something with which employees can identify, and with pride. It is here that the clear mission statements described in Chapter four come into their own, providing a rallying cry that can help foster a sense of belonging and corporate pride.

Keeping it useful

Local government has an unenviable habit of going overboard in the way it implements good ideas picked up from elsewhere. Such a conclusion certainly emerges from a study of local government's experiences with corporate planning. There is therefore a danger that strategic planning may be pursued by some people as if it were an end in itself, rather than merely a means to the end of delivering services to the community. If this were to happen, one of the first casualties would be support from service department officers. For, as has already been identified, one of the most telling objections to participation in processes such as strategic planning is the amount of time it requires to be diverted from managing day-to-day service delivery. The need to retain the commitment of service department officers suggests that two qualities are of particular importance in a strategic plan:

▽ **relevance** It must be widely seen as a worthwhile investment of scarce time and energy, with clear benefits for the authority as a whole, individual services, and individual officers. This is unlikely to be so if it degenerates into a mechanistic approach.

▽ **brevity** It has been said that strategic plans become less and less useful as they get bigger and bigger and as more and more hours go into preparing them. The point at which that starts to be true may well vary between different authorities; but the lessons of corporate planning suggest that there is a lot of truth in the generalisation.

Experience suggests that one of the results of getting to grips with management development is that managers are increasingly to be heard pushing for clearer guidance on where the authority is heading. There can be no clearer proof that officers see strategic planning as a benefit to them. It is, after all, in their interest as much as anyone's to see that the organisation is on the right lines.

Review questions

▲ How far does your authority waste effort through lack of planning and
   co-ordination?
▲ How far are your authority's officers encouraged to think beyond their
   specific job?
▲ How much do they know about what the local authority is trying to
   achieve?
▲ How much do they know of what is expected of them?
▲ How do they assess whether they are doing a good job?
▲ Is there a clear sense of direction for the authority with which employees
   can identify?

10 How does the community benefit?

Key points

▲ Local authorities are judged principally by the excellence and efficiency of their services.

▲ For strategic planning to be worthwhile, it must make a significant contribution towards attaining those qualities.

▲ And people — as customers — must benefit.

▲ But people should benefit as citizens also.

Contributing to better services

One of the basic assumptions underlying strategic planning is that people who use local government's services — its customers — get a better deal from local authorities that:

▽ have a clear view of the direction they want to move in
▽ have resolved their priorities
▽ have thought through the structure of the organisation needed to achieve them.

But that assumption remains largely untested. Is there evidence to demonstrate that strategic planning really does help to improve quality and mean better services for customers?

The answer should be 'yes'.

The fundamental elements of strategic planning provide the ingredients to do so, for instance:

▽ the clear sense of purpose and direction that is evident in the City of Birmingham's statement of its economic resurgence through initiatives such as the International Convention Centre and its bid for the Olympic Games

▽ the facility to innovate and experiment that characterises the 'PIRATE' project in rural Devon — bringing library and information services to sparsely-populated areas

▽ the resilience that is enabling some authorities to plan and carry through a process of radical change in education with remarkable smoothness in the face of daunting pressures from legislation

▽ the purposeful progress, revealed by surveying customers' views, that has been achieved in the improvement of education and housing services in the London Borough of Richmond-upon-Thames

▽   the targeting of priority action evident in the emphasis that Wrekin District Council has placed on overcoming people's concerns about vandalism.

But overall does strategic planning bring real benefits to the person in the street?

The experts' view

There is no doubt where the experts stand. The Audit Commission (in 'The Competitive Council') described the well-managed council as one that:

▽   understands its customers
▽   responds to the electorate
▽   sets and pursues consistent, achievable objectives
▽   assigns clear management responsibilities
▽   trains and motivates people
▽   communicates effectively
▽   monitors results
▽   adapts to change.

The theme of strategic planning runs through all of these 'key success factors'.

Not unnaturally, the message is one that is taken up in advice by management consultants and external auditors, and reverberates round local authorities. Their views are perhaps best summed up in the external auditors' management letter to one council, where they criticised the absence of an overall strategic plan for the authority and recommended that: '(1) the Authority develops measurable objectives for individual committees and for the Council as a whole; (2) these objectives should be incorporated in the development of a brief strategic plan for the Authority'.

Strategic planning has therefore penetrated deep into the management consultants' psyche, and is a recurring feature of the advice on improving the management of local authorities. The link between better management and better services is seen as self-evident, and perhaps is. The true test, however, is whether the customers are more satisfied and feel they are getting better services.

The customers' view

We have come across no study of customer satisfaction comparing local authorities which practise strategic planning with those that do not. The evidence available is therefore anecdotal. But that evidence comes down firmly in favour of strategic planning. Two examples more than make the point.

In Warwickshire County Council, the switch in emphasis from residential to community care for elderly people emerged from a strategic review in the late 1970s. That review — entitled 'Your Own Front Door' — took as its starting point the wishes of elderly people. Those wishes became very clear — the overwhelming preference of elderly people was to remain in their own homes with support from home care and other services rather than sacrifice their independence through admission to 'old peoples' homes'.

Out of that review was born a policy which:

▽ stimulated the development of very sheltered housing in co-operation with district councils. Through an agreed formula, the County Council met the extra costs of the community facilities that enhanced 'sheltered housing' into 'very sheltered housing'. As a result, there are now 792 very sheltered homes throughout the county.

▽ expanded community support facilities so that the Council's home care, telephone, meals, and other support services now outstrip those of most other counties — by conscious decision.

▽ resulted in elderly people 'voting with their feet', and staying in their own homes, so that despite an increase of nearly 30% in their numbers over the past 10 years, the County Council has been able to close one home for elderly people and by reducing places from 1032 to 768 to provide many more single rooms and improved facilities in the remaining homes. Despite this, there is effectively no waiting list for admission to homes for elderly people.

Sheffield City Council's Libraries and Information Services department introduced strategic planning into its management process in the mid 1980s. Sections in the department produce forward plans setting out:

▽ aims and objectives
▽ targets
▽ priorities
▽ performance.

This clearly-structured process has made the battery of improvements introduced for all groups of library users easy to trace — leading in particular to higher use by very young and elderly people, while longer day-time opening has led to more people borrowing books.

Of course, it is possible to argue that these improvements were attributable to factors other than the more systematic approach to management injected by strategic planning. The contrast between Sheffield libraries' success and the comparative failure of another library service — where strategic planning was notable by its absence — perhaps counters that point. In the latter case, survey evidence collected by consultants revealed that only one-half of residents made use of the library service, and that the most significant factor inhibiting wider use was the pattern of day-time opening.

Passing the customer test

These two examples suggest that strategic planning does pass the 'customer relevance' test. It is not just the management consultants' 'flavour of the month', but a management technique that brings real improvements in services to customers. Local government is largely a service industry. Unless it satisfies its customers, it will wither into irrelevance — and will deserve to. The spread of strategic planning will help prevent that.

This book has been primarily concerned with strategic planning as an authority-wide activity. By contrast, the examples in this chapter are concerned with the effects of strategic planning within individual services. That benefit to customers should be most easily illustrated in this way is hardly surprising, since it is improvements at the sharp end that have the most obvious impact on the users of services.

However, it should not be concluded that there are no customer benefits from authority-wide strategic planning. On the contrary: it is frequently strategic planning for the organisation as a whole that leads to strategic planning in individual services. And where the latter exists without the former, strategic planning in a particular service takes place in the absence of an authority overview, and runs the risk of ending up as a plan without resources allocated to back it.

Passing the citizen test

So far in this chapter, the emphasis has been on members of the public as customers, for the simple reason that it is from the standpoint of consumers of services that most members of the public judge their local authority. But the community is more than a collection of consumers: people are also residents or workers in the area governed by a council; voters; ratepayers or community charge payers — in other words, citizens. What has strategic planning to offer them?

In fact, it is as citizens even more than as customers that the public benefits from some of the examples already quoted. For example, relatively few people from Birmingham may use the new International Convention Centre. But there will be many who gain from a burgeoning feeling of pride in their city, recalling the civic confidence of the days of the Chamberlain family.

Nor is the benefit to the community of strategic planning all so intangible. In the case of Birmingham, very many people will benefit from the spin-offs in the local economy. And, more generally, ratepayers and community charge payers of authorities that have got to grips with strategic planning can be confident that their money is not being squandered on:

∇   services working against each other
∇   services duplicating each other
∇   needless reversals of policy
∇   activities aborted for lack of proper planning
∇   last-minute panic measures

and all the other trappings of reactive administration as opposed to strategic management.

Review questions

▲   What examples are there in your authority of strategic planning bringing identifiable benefits to customers?
▲   How far does it display the Audit Commission's key success factors of understanding its customers and responding to the electorate?
▲   Does it have a sense of direction with which the local community identifies?

11 Getting the act together

Key points

▲ Some local authorities are clearly making a success of strategic planning.
▲ However, some impressive-looking processes are actually achieving little.
▲ Success is more likely where emphasis is put on developing a strategic culture rather than just on mechanistic processes.

Successes and difficulties

'Senior officers and members were, and still are, very much committed to the concept and to the document itself.'

'The gains have been enormous ... Attitudes and public comments of members, while guarded about what the future may hold, have been very supportive about the principles ... and what has been achieved in the recent processes.'

'... there remains all-party support for the approach we have adopted ... (it) has become an accepted part of the Council's vocabulary.'

'... we have by encouragement and persuasion achieved a corporately-owned exercise which has the enthusiastic endorsement of members.'

We came across the above comments, and others like them, in preparing this book. Given such successes, and the examples we quote in earlier chapters, how can we assert (as we did in Chapter one) that notable examples of strategic planning are not widespread? The reason for this apparent discrepancy is that, in our view, with some authorities there is — to coin a phrase — less to it than meets the eye!

It is not hard to come by examples of the output of strategic planning processes, and they are often superficially impressive. A cursory glance can suggest rigorous systems, carefully thought out procedures, well structured documents. But, all too frequently, deeper probing reveals one or more of the following ailments, any of which can deal a death blow to successful progress. We have come across them all.

LITTLE INFLUENCE ON COUNCILLORS

One officer sent a genuinely impressive document, but stated that: 'If I were

honest, I would have to say that members have not taken wholeheartedly to the
... process'.

As long as councillors see a strategic plan as irrelevant, or — even worse —
unwelcome, it will achieve little or nothing. It will be ignored when important
decisions are taken, instead of providing a framework of guidance for such
decisions. The problem may lie in the plan's content, particularly if the agenda
is an officer-led rather than a political one. Or it may be in the process that the
difficulty lies, particularly if councillors have simply not accepted the value of a
strategic approach. There is no single route to follow, and success can never be
guaranteed. At the end of the day, the proverbial horse cannot always be
enticed into drinking. But what can be said with confidence is that failure is all
but assured if strenuous efforts are not made to:

▽   involve councillors fully and from an early stage
▽   address their concerns
▽   gain their 'ownership' of the process and its output
▽   produce something that is not just relevant but intelligible and usable.

LITTLE INTEREST BEYOND THE CENTRE

'To be honest, we (at the centre) are finding introducing a clearer policy
process hard work....'

All too often, it appears that the only people committed to the process are
officers in a central department, vainly struggling to impose on reluctant (or
even hostile) service departments a process for which the latter have no
enthusiasm. This may arise from an inappropriate process, or it may reflect
short-sightedness on the part of service departments. Either way, it spells
trouble.

There is, of course, no getting away from the fundamental truth that the
centre of an organisation is ultimately responsible for an organisation-wide
strategy; but it is a rare — and unhealthy? — organisation that has a centre so
powerful that it can impose a strategy or strategy-making process without
persuasion. And it is a misguided centre that fails to take service departments'
perspectives into account in devising a process in the first place.

LOSS OF MOMENTUM

There are many reasons for not being able to keep going. Amongst those most
commonly encountered are:

▽   **weight of paper**
    'The updating process raised less enthusiasm than the initial production.
    Additionally, concern was expressed at the large quantities of paper ... the
    exercise lost impetus and to some extent credibility.'

    Local government delivers a wide range of services, each one of which
    embraces a number of important areas of change. There are relatively few
    areas where things can just be left to tick over, in the current challenging
    climate. It is therefore understandable that some authorities find it hard to
    be selective, and to limit their focus in devising strategies. But a
    comprehensive approach can so quickly become self-defeating, with the
    amount of paper choking off any enthusiasm and causing the process to
    grind to a halt, with much of the written material remaining unread.

▽ **burden of work**
'The strategic plan ... foundered due to lack of staff resources, and, perhaps, a gradually increasing awareness of the enormity of the task.'

Strategies cannot be devised without effort. And, as has been suggested, that effort has to involve councillors and service department officers, who will invariably have their own preoccupations. The real key to success must be to ensure that managers embrace strategic thinking as part of their job, and see strategic planning as something that helps and supports them in that job. Emphasising the process of strategic planning rather than the philosophy will simply make it a burden that puts active and willing participation at risk.

DEPENDENCE ON GROWTH

'... not progressed because the various growth elements ... could not be financed within the financial constraints of the Council ...'

Many processes, particularly those that are based on a 'bottom-up' approach, fail to provide corporate guidance on the direction of change, or on the likely scale of resources available. The result can all too easily be enthusiasm on the part of service departments — but enthusiasm for a process seen as providing an opportunity to press for extra resources. When resources are scarce, such a process can quickly lose all credibility.

LACK OF LINKS WITH BUDGET

'It was considered that, on its own, strategic planning could become an "objective-setting" exercise, lacking financial realism ... The integrated approach ... was never achieved.'

Some authorities operate a process that combines strategic planning and budgeting. This can take the form of (say) a three-year budget where the annual roll-forward reflects decisions of a strategic nature about the authority's overall direction and its priorities. This, however, is not the only route: other authorities consciously separate the two elements on the grounds that strategic decision-making should be kept apart from the hurried, pragmatic decision-making so often associated with budget time. The latter course can work — but only if there is a clear way of ensuring that strategic decisions are actually fed into the budget process in some way or other. A clear link by no means always exists.

MISSING THE GENUINELY STRATEGIC

It is central to the thesis of this book that strategic planning requires an authority-wide perspective and a focus on change. For a surprising number of authorities, what are termed strategic plans turn out to be little more than the bringing together of service plans, with little to link them, draw out common threads, or establish priorities. And even where service plans are prefaced with a corporate context, this can be of a very static nature, reflecting a traditional outlook rather than emphasising a changing order. It seems that, for some authorities, the link between a generalised mission statement and a detailed action plan is hard to define — yet that is exactly what strategy is all about.

The nub of the issue

The above quotations and causes of difficulty are not intended to be discouraging. (It may actually prove comforting for those who are struggling to see that others share the same predicament!) Nor are they meant as criticisms: we have yet to come across anyone who claims that success in strategic planning in local government is easily won. Indeed, one chief executive wrote: 'There will be future failures because we ... believe in a lot of innovation and the bouncing off of a lot of ideas ... we have to make mistakes to move forward...'.

However, it is hard to avoid the conclusion that some of the mistakes of the corporate planning era of the 1960s and 1970s are being repeated. Above all, there does appear to be a lot of emphasis on the mechanics and a relative neglect of the underlying culture. As the examples quoted earlier show, a technically impressive strategic plan can fail for want of support. By contrast, a strategic vision can be successfully translated into action without there actually being a written strategy document. As one chief executive commented, 'Any strategic document is secondary to the process'.

We are not actually advocating doing without a document. Without the discipline of producing a tangible output, strategic planning as a process is unlikely to become well established in most settings. But the moral is clear: the style, approach, and vision of the local authority are more important than the bare achievement of producing a strategic plan. And strategic style, approach, and vision will be reflected in other aspects of strategic management (as described in Chapter six) as well as in strategic planning.

The triumph of strategic culture over the mechanistic approach is summed up admirably by proposals emanating from one authority, whose previous attempts had run into difficulties:

'It is proposed that emphasis be placed on ... a strategic planning *process* rather than ... a corporate planning *document*. The output of the process would be a bundle of consistent, comprehensive, and well targeted "policy vehicles" ... e.g. the annual budget, the Transport Policy and Programme, the Unitary Development Plan, the Housing Investment Programme, the Council's economic strategy, etc. ... These would be prepared so that each is consciously orientated to the achievement of the Council's strategic objectives.'

That sounds like real planning for change.

References

General

Audit Commission 1983 *Improving Economy, Efficiency, and Effectiveness in Local Government in England and Wales*. Vol. 1

Audit Commission 1988 *The Competitive Council*. HMSO

Audit Commission 1988 *Performance Review in Local Government — Action Guide*. HMSO

Barratt J. 1987 *Strategic Management in Local Government*. Unpublished

Bichard M. 1989 'Management today needs a new style' *Local Government Chronicle* (20 January)

Clarke M. and Stewart J. 1988 *Managing Tomorrow*. LGTB

Clarke M. and Stewart J. 1988 *The Enabling Council — developing and managing a new style of local government*. LGTB

Community Care: Agenda for Action. 1988 (Griffiths Report), HMSO

Coopers and Lybrand 1988 *Local Management of Schools*. Crown Copyright

Corrigan P. et al 1988 *Socialism, Merit, and Efficiency*. Fabian Society

Development Plans — a manual of form and content. 1971 HMSO

District Audit Service 1986 *Value for Money in Northumberland*

Eddison T. 1973 *Local Government- Management and Corporate Planning* Leonard Hill

Eiles C. and Ellsworth R. 1988 'Performance in review — an activity for managers not councillors' *Local Government Chronicle*. (19 August)

Going for Better Management — a strategic approach to management development. 1988 LGTB

Kinsley Lord 1989 *Cambridgeshire Council Council: Into the 1990s*.

Latham D. 1988 'Climate for Change' *County Councils Gazette*. (August)

Quinn 1980 *Strategies for Change*. Irwin

Report of the Committee on Management of Local Government. 1967 (Maud Report), HMSO

Ridley N. 1988 *The Local Right — enabling not providing*. Centre for Policy Studies

Stewart J. 1986 *Strategic Management in Local Government*. LGTB

Taylor W. 1988 'Performance review is essential in today's world' *Municipal Journal*. (23 September)

The Conduct of Local Authority Business. 1986 (Widdicombe Report), HMSO

The Future of Development Plans — a consultation paper. 1986 DOE/Welsh Office

The Future of Development Plans. 1989 HMSO

The New Local Authorities - management and structure. 1972 (Bains Report), HMSO

Ward F.W. 1984 'Policy Planning at Grimsby' *Local Government Chronicle*.

Local authority documents

Arun District Council 1988 *Framework of Overall Arrangements for the Effective and Efficient Management of its Business Affairs*.

Arun District Council 1987 *Strategy Papers and Programme Plans 1987–91*.

Avon County Council 1987 *Guidelines for completing Position Statement Forms*.

Berkshire County Council 1988 *Medium Term Planning 1989–92*.

Bexley London Borough Council *The Business Process*.

Bradford City Council 1987 *The Social Strategy in Action*.

Braintree District Council 1985 *The Way Forward*.

Braintree District Council 1986 *The Way Forward: Policy Objectives and Plans*

Cambridgeshire County Council 1987 *Medium Term Plan 1989–92: Information Digest* (includes Ten Year Outlook).

Cambridgeshire County Council 1988 *Corporate Planning in Cambridgeshire: A Position Statement – Autumn 1988*.

Cheshire County Council *Mission Statement*.

Cheshire County Countil 1988 *Strategic Management Review: Reveiw of the County Council's Management Structure*.

Coventry City Council *Contact*.

Devon County Council *Public Information in Rural Areas Technology Experiment*. (PIRATE)

Gloucestershire County Council 1988 *Gloucestershire Review 1988*.

Hampshire County Council 1987 *Key Areas for Achievement 1987–9*.

Northamptonshire County Council 1988 *Medium Term Plan 1988–91*.

Northumberland County Council 1987 *Service Assessment and Review*.

Richmond upon Thames London Borough Council 1988 *Operational Plan 1988/9–1989/90*.

Sheffield City Council 1988 *Forward Plans.* (Libraries and Information Services)

Suffolk County Council 1988 *Medium Term Strategic Plan 1988–92.*

Suffolk County Council 1986 *Service Priority Review: a manual for members and officers.*

Thamesdown Borough Council 1984 *A New Vision for Thamesdown — A Consultation Document.*

Thamesdown Borough Council 1985 *A New Vision for Thamesdown — Strategy Statement.*

Wansdyke District Council 1987 *Management Changes.*

Warwickshire County Council 1989 *The Challenges Ahead: Strategic Issues facing the County Council.*

Warwickshire County Council 1980 *Your Own Front Door.*

Wiltshire County Council 1988 *Codification and Revision of the County Council's Management Process.*

Wiltshire County Council 1988 *The Role of Members.*

Windsor and Maidenhead Royal Borough Council 1986 *Way Ahead.*

Wrekin District Council 1988 *Priorities Report 1989–92.*

Index